BoardSteps ©

The Framework for
Effective Nonprofit Governance

Joann Morgan Burstein

Nonprofit Board Advisors, LLC

Philadelphia · Denver

For information, contact
Nonprofit Board Advisors, LLC
1820 Rittenhouse Square, Suite 1102
Philadelphia, PA 19103
215-893-7887
www.boardsteps.com

Burstein, Joann Morgan
    BoardSteps : the framework for effective nonprofit
governance / Joann Morgan Burstein.
    p. cm.
    Includes bibliographical references.
    LCCN 2004098323
    ISBN 0-9745418-4-2

    1. Nonprofit organizations–Management. 2. Boards
of directors. I. Title.

HD62.6.B877 2003   658'.048
                             QBI03-200835

Production Management by
Paros Press
1551 Larimer Street, Suite 1301   Denver, CO 80202
303-893-3332   www.parospress.com

BOOK DESIGN BY SCOTT JOHNSON

Printed in the United States of America
1 3 5 7 9 10 8 6 4 2

Contents

This book is dedicated to the directors

of the many nonprofits that struggle to achieve

maximum results with minimal budgets.

BoardSteps is designed to help your board

become a more effective contributor

to your organization and community.

Foreword

"The noblest question in the world," Ben Franklin wrote, "is 'What good can I do in it?'"

Not-for-profit organizations help millions of Americans answer that question every day. Concentrating on people and how their lives are woven together to form the fabric of communities, nonprofits satisfy essential human needs for those who receive their services—and for those who help provide them.

A successful nonprofit benefits from the collective vision, creativity and determination of many people. At the same time, each individual— whether staff or volunteer—benefits from the experience of working with others in pursuit of a common purpose and desired results.

Nowhere is this cooperative experience more rewarding—or more important for the organization—than on the board of directors where a unique kind of volunteer leader is responsible not only for serving but also for governing. By accepting this added responsibility, a director pledges to keep the nonprofit focused on its mission, sound in its finances, ethical and efficient in its operations, and vibrant in its capacity for growth and transformation.

Yet personal passion and commitment (and consistent attendance at meetings!) take a director only so far. Serving on a board without formal orientation and education is like joining an orchestra without being trained to play an instrument. Initially the excitement is palpable, but as time goes on it becomes clear that the skills are not sufficient to contribute meaningfully to the performance.

Lack of formal training is just as apparent at the board table as on the orchestra stage. Many an eager director has approached the position full of promise and ideas, only to grow frustrated in the absence of clear instructions, expectations, and lines of communication. It takes more than dedication to the cause to reap the rewards of board service. To be competent at its job, a board must first be educated about the science of governance in order to practice the art of it.

The vital, yet poorly understood function of a nonprofit board has fascinated me for more than twenty-five years. From my first board appointment, I have been motivated to learn more about what it means to practice good governance. I read, attended seminars, was mentored by several outstanding directors, and in turn, mentored others. Many of my friends in the nonprofit sector—board members, funders, executive directors and staff— were constantly looking for ways to strengthen boards and they came to me for help. So my consulting career was launched.

> "The noblest question in the world is 'What good can I do in it?'"
>
> Benjamin Franklin

BoardSteps delivers a conceptual framework for understanding the role of the board.

No text can prepare a consultant for the nuances that make each organization unique. However, confusion about what directors should be doing at the board table is common. I have come to realize that step-by-step details of the governance function can help a board feel good about its contribution while demonstrating accountability to the public.

That is where this book comes in. **BoardSteps** delivers a conceptual framework for understanding the role of the board, and concrete guidance in creating structures that allow directors to fulfill their governance responsibilities for the health of the nonprofit and the community it serves.

Now more than ever, the times call for change. Economic globalization, political uncertainty, and changing attitudes about the independent sector have amplified a host of major issues that must be addressed first at the board level:

◆ **Funder Accountability.** Grantors and donors increasingly demand detailed reporting of measurable results.

◆ **Public Accountability.** Intensifying media reports of poor board oversight and lack of transparency make proper governance a must.

◆ **New Funding Approaches.** Entrepreneurial fund-raising ventures (e.g. the formation of for-profit subsidiaries) invite greater scrutiny by concerned donors, as well as, local, state and federal taxing authorities.

◆ **New Technology.** The online world provides new avenues for board collaboration and easier access to information by the public. Boards must help their organizations respond to, and take advantage of, advanced technologies and changes driven by the Internet.

Nonprofit boards are always faced with multiple challenges and opportunities. To succeed in this environment, each director must make a personal commitment to learn about the job and the accompanying liabilities. As a whole, the board must develop the capacity to govern systematically, fairly and strategically. Investing organizational resources on training today will improve board performance and enhance the nonprofit's societal impact tomorrow. I hope that this book will provide you and your board with the governance tools to position your organization for success.

Joann Morgan Burstein

Introduction to BoardSteps

Why Do We Need a Board Governance Framework?

"Social advance," wrote Jane Addams, "depends as much upon the process through which it is secured as upon the result itself."

Building on that premise, a nonprofit organization needs an effective system of governance if it is to prosper. During my years as a director, staffer and consultant in the independent sector, I have experienced the importance of structures that allow boards to exercise due diligence and engage in strategic planning. I have also observed what happens when such structures are not in place. The enthusiasm of many new directors is quickly replaced with frustration because no one tells them what they are supposed to be doing and how to do it. So the myth of "learning by doing" at the board table is just that: a myth.

Countless boards believe that governing means reviewing staff tasks and attending to line-by-line management details. This is a natural response because many directors bring this mentality from their professional lives. However, with this mindset, the crucial work of governance goes undone. While education and planning should be on every board agenda, more often than not, pressing operational issues become the priority. There is never enough time to attend to the principal part the board should play in the nonprofit's community impact.

Specifically, a board that shares a clear definition of its job is able to contribute positively to organizational performance. It maintains focus on long-term results, discharges its legal and fiduciary obligations, and proactively manages a smooth succession of board leadership as experienced members step down and new members fill their seats.

Every nonprofit, whether it is brand new or celebrating its centennial, needs a governance model. Over the years, I have listened to directors around the country complain about uncertainties surrounding their responsibilities. They share similar worries about what they

> A board that shares a clear definition of its job is able to contribute positively to organizational performance.

1

should be doing to prove accountability. And while volumes have been written about management, help for the board side of the equation is in limited supply.

BoardSteps contributes to the growing body of knowledge on board governance. The core of the framework stems from the basic conviction that **Results equals Relationships plus Resources.** Human *relationships* form the inspiration, purpose and engine of every nonprofit. *Resources[1]* make the work of a nonprofit possible. A strategic joining of intentional relationships and leveraging of available resources produces positive *results* that advance the organization's mission.

Results = Relationships + Resources

This book outlines a process that...

◆ Allows the organization's leadership to be strategic in its thinking and planning as it examines available data to build future scenarios.

◆ Puts in place a checklist to ensure legal compliance.

◆ Looks intensively at how governance and management functions intermesh to concentrate organizational efforts.

◆ Recognizes that no framework is worth the paper it's printed on unless it can be easily understood and implemented without consuming large quantities of a board's already limited time.

So What is Governance?

A cursory look in any dictionary tells us that governance is the process of making policy and administering affairs with sovereign authority. In a nonprofit corporation, the board has sovereign authority—or, as Harry Truman put it, *The Buck Stops Here.* While individual directors may come and go, the board as a collective entity has both the power and the responsibility to craft the vision and principles that drive organizational actions. In order to govern, the board must meet in formal sessions to make corporate decisions, and it should communicate those decisions to the staff and the public in what John Carver (1990)

[1] Resources: The general term used to include financial, human and in-kind resources.

terms "a single voice." Put simply, the board is the legal reason the non-profit can exist.[2]

As for policy and administration, the Preamble of the U.S. Constitution reminds us that good government should "establish Justice, insure domestic Tranquility, provide for the common Defence" and "promote the general Welfare." So too, the board of a nonprofit is legally and ethically charged with formulating fair and rational policies, laying the foundation for smooth operations, protecting the corporation's assets, and articulating a clear mission that contributes to the well-being of the community.

The actual practice of board governance has legal, regulatory, innovative, and evaluative components. First, to protect the public interest, the board makes sure the nonprofit functions within the lawful parameters prescribed by federal, state and local governments. Second, it demands efficient and ethical practices at all levels of the organization. Third, it determines the nonprofit's strategic direction by continually weighing external forces and internal realities. Finally, it sets standards by which the organization's performance and progress may be monitored.

Standards are the Key

This last component, the setting of standards, is worthy of particular emphasis. In this fundamental governance exercise, the board's collective wisdom is synthesized into and expressed through measurable statements. Standards are critical to good governance, and yet they are the least understood of all the components.

So what is a standard? A standard is the board's final word about what it expects to happen over a certain period of time. It measures individual and organizational behavior according to clear, familiar concepts: quantity, quality and degree. Standards are the rules by which the organization, board and staff conduct business. Two examples:

◆ A board may determine that each director should attend a stated number of meetings per year, serve on a board committee, and contribute a certain amount of money to the organization annually. In so doing, the board sets a performance standard for its members.

Positive results are a product of intentional relationships and available resources.

[2] This book is written for and about boards and does not address the area of management infrastructure.

3

◆ A board may mandate a specific percentage of organizational revenue to achieve a particular outcome. In that case, the board sets a quantifiable standard for the value the organization gives to both its funders and its clients. The executive is left to make the standard an operational reality, and to develop a reporting mechanism that allows the board to ensure compliance.

As these examples illustrate, efficient nonprofit operations start with good ideas about how to run an organization, but standards turn good ideas into sound governance. Standards allow the board to ascertain that it is doing its job lawfully, and to demonstrate that the nonprofit contributes positively to the community. A board faces few challenges greater than the development of clear and comprehensive standards.

Once standards are established, the next hurdle is the manner in which a board utilizes them. Some boards have no logical system at all, with policies dispersed among old meeting minutes and the memories of certain individual directors. Some have an incomplete set, while others adopt standards that are excessively vague, unenforceable, or impossible to measure. Still others enact standards piecemeal, in reaction to crises that reveal an urgent need for them. And the most ineffective board is the one that establishes standards by doing nothing. Its inaction produces two possible paths. Either the organization will stagnate with no direction or management will set the standards by any actions it chooses. It is sadly apparent that this kind of board has abandoned its responsibility and adds no value to the work of the nonprofit or the sector.

In contrast, **BoardSteps** advocates a methodical creation and implementation of standards to prevent organizational problems from arising in the first place. The framework requires that written, measurable standards be articulated in a deliberate, proactive manner. And these standards then relate to one another in a clear, organized fashion, forming a coherent system of governance. Monitoring must occur regularly: a portion of each board meeting agenda should be dedicated exclusively to objective monitoring, without bias toward or against the particular players involved in a given situation.

BoardSteps also encourages an awareness of the different levels of standard setting that take place in even the smallest organizations. The board should concern itself with organizational standards, while the executive should write operational standards. In the second exam-

> **A board faces few challenges greater than the development of clear and comprehensive standards.**

4

ple shared earlier, the board sets a standard for service and efficiency, while the executive determines how to meet it, in part by instituting a number of more intermediate standards that direct the staff's day-to-day activities. As your board works through this book, you will have an opportunity to make the necessary distinctions between these different levels of standard setting.

Any board, no matter what its level of sophistication, can use the **BoardSteps** process to focus organizational responsibilities and establish standards to gauge effectiveness.

While one board may be comfortable with a few broad standards, another will want to express its collective wisdom in more depth. This is the board's prerogative and it must be satisfied that it is providing clear guidance for all nonprofit actions. The board practices good governance by engaging in a deliberative exercise to set direction and formulate checks and balances.

Establishing standards takes time! The standard-writing process requires discipline and attention to detail. For this reason, some directors would prefer to dedicate as little time as possible to this task because it creates a feeling of distance from the caring work of the nonprofit. However, once standards have been written and monitoring mechanisms activated, the organization runs more smoothly—and the board actually finds itself with more time to concentrate on supporting the nonprofit's core purpose and on positioning the organization for upcoming opportunities.

Establishing standards takes time!

The BoardSteps Process: How to Use This Book

This book is organized into three sections intended to help boards work through the process of instituting **BoardSteps**.

Section 1 consists of this **Introduction**, which explains the rationale for this book, discusses the importance of board governance and sketches the basics of the framework.

Section 2, **Practicing BoardSteps**, focuses on the actual process of setting up a governance structure through identification and pursuit of desired *results*, essential *relationships*, and existing and potential *resources*.

We will cover the process at two distinct levels in six steps:

Governance
at the
organizational
level shapes
the nonprofit's
external face as
it interacts with
funders, clients
and the general
public.

◆ The *organizational level,* in which the board and the executive collaborate to define desirable and attainable results, and develop an appropriate division of labor and responsibility; and

◆ The *board level,* in which the board establishes the proper infrastructure and working relationships necessary for it to act responsibly and ultimately demonstrate accountability.

It is helpful to remember that these two levels correspond to a nonprofit's two main dimensions: governance at the organizational level shapes the nonprofit's external face as it interacts with funders, clients and the general public. In contrast, at the board level, the board configures its internal support system to underpin the practice of good governance. The importance and dynamics of results, relationships and resources of each level are highlighted throughout the book. A series of worksheets guides the process.

Section 3, **Standards, Worksheets, and References**, addresses the development of standards, presents worksheets that supplement Section Two, and notes references. The **BoardSteps** job description is located at the end of this section.

By consulting the material and worksheets in all three sections of this book, a board can assemble the building blocks of a governance system appropriate to its particular organization. I encourage directors to read the entire book before beginning the **BoardSteps** process. In that way, your board will have an appreciation of the whole framework and your work will be more meaningful.

A Note on Terminology

Like any field, the nonprofit world is saturated with jargon. Over time the meanings of many of these terms have become muddled and the distinctions among them unclear.

The following groupings list terms that have similar meanings. For clarity's sake, **BoardSteps** will only use the one or two words in bold print at the beginning of each group.

◆ *Nonprofit (Not-for-profit, NPO, Tax-exempt Corporation, Public Charity, Service Organization, Aid Society, Agency, Non-governmental Organization, NGO)*

◆ *Nonprofit Sector (Independent Sector, Third Sector, NGO Sector)*
A variety of terms describe the sort of enterprise for which this book has been written, and the area of influence in which it operates. All such organizations are united by their legal status as corporations that do not earn profits and do not usually pay income taxes; and by the prioritization of outcomes other than profit making. For these reasons, the term *nonprofit* designates such organizations and *nonprofit sector* denotes the economic, political and social sphere of operation.

◆ *Director, Board Member (Trustee, Overseer, Governor)*

◆ *Board (Board of Directors, Board of Trustees, Board of Overseers, Governing Committee)*
Legally, one serves on a board as a director. As the *Guidebook for Directors of Nonprofit Corporations* (American Bar Association) explains, "Every nonprofit corporation statute provides for a board of directors; but, in a given corporation, the name of this body varies with the history, tradition—and whim—of the organization involved." **BoardSteps** employs two of the most commonly used terms—*director* and *board member*—to refer to individuals who serve on a nonprofit's governing body. The generic term *board* refers to that body.

◆ *Client (Recipient, Customer, Consumer, Participant, User of Services)*
Those served by nonprofits are variously designated by the nature of the organization's mission. The *Drucker Foundation Self-Assessment Tool* addresses these descriptors in a simple way: "Who must be satisfied for the organization to achieve results? When you answer this question, you define your customer as one who values your service, who wants what you offer, who feels it's important to *them.*" *Client* designates the recipient of a nonprofit's programs and services.

◆ *Executive* (*Executive Director, CEO, President, Staff Coordinator, Designated Staff Leader, Manager*)

◆ *Management, Staff* (*Employees, Associates, Assistants*)

The person who occupies the top position in an organization's staff hierarchy is the board's only employee, the *executive*. Other *staff* is hired and managed by the executive. *Management* indicates the non-board side of the organization in general.

◆ *Workgroup* (*Committee, Task Force, Ad Hoc Committee*)

This term refers to any group the board charges with accomplishing tasks and reporting back to the board. The board must make certain that each board committee functions at the governance level and is not doing a management job. Responsiveness and flexibility are key. In some cases a permanent standing committee, such as board development, is necessary to address ongoing governance responsibilities. In other situations it is more efficient to appoint a temporary ad hoc group with a distinct charge that is dissolved when its task is completed. To cover both types of arrangements, this book employs the generic term *workgroup* — a group assigned to do certain work.

◆ *Standard* (*Policy, Procedure, Goal, Objective, Benchmark, Evaluation Tool, Performance Measure*)

Nonprofits use many terms in the course of organizational planning, administration and evaluation. **BoardSteps** uses the general term *standard* because it encompasses the more precise meanings of the other terms. Sticking with the most general term acknowledges the fact that *each board must decide for itself what particular kinds of standards* to institute for different facets of the organization and its operations. Ultimately, it is the board's responsibility to know what each standard measures and why.

◆ *Governing Documents*

When a nonprofit chooses to incorporate, it must make application to its state government. Articles of Incorporation outline the conditions that must be met to obtain the not-for-profit corporation designation. Bylaws, a set of rules, prescribe how the organization will manage its affairs. Most states outline what will be in these two legal documents that then provide the umbrella for organizational standards.

Practicing BoardSteps

Results = Relationships + Resources

BoardSteps offers a simple formula: **Results equals Relationships plus Resources.** It proceeds from the equally simple assumption that a nonprofit exists to benefit the community. The first question that must be asked, then, is:

What results will be produced?

An organization must ask itself what it wants to accomplish before it can determine what it will do or how it will do it. What value will it add for the greater good? How will attitudes, behaviors or institutions change, and how will lives be enriched or transformed because of organizational activities? In short, what differences will the nonprofit make in its community?

R = R + R
RESULTS What results will be produced?
RELATIONSHIPS What relationships are necessary to achieve the results?
RESOURCES What resources are needed to support the results?

After results, the other two areas must be defined:

What relationships are necessary to achieve the results?

The nonprofit sector is fundamentally about people uniting to reach a common goal. A nonprofit operates through any number of linkages within the organization and with outside individuals and institutions. A board must recognize, cultivate and sustain these relationships to promote the organization's results.

BoardSteps offers a simple formula: Results equals Relationships plus Resources.

What resources are needed to support the results?

Financial resources, of course, are pivotal to realizing results. To fulfill its legal and ethical obligations, a board must stipulate financial needs, and then pursue and allocate resources in a manner directly tied to the mission and preferred organizational outcomes. With **BoardSteps**, resources are always considered financial, encompassing both human and in-kind resources.

Results = Relationships + Resources = Results

The attentive reader will note that the **BoardSteps** equation moves in both directions. In day-to-day operations, the organization builds relationships and seeks the financial resources necessary to obtain the desired results—we are all familiar with that kind of work. At the same time, however, results dictate what kinds of relationships and funding resources are required. The board must specify the results it wants, then continually monitor performance in pursuit of those results. In addition, it periodically revisits the mission to see if external conditions in the community and the wider world require changes in its strategic positioning choices.

This seesaw nature of the framework is like cultivating a garden. Ideally, we first determine what plants we want to grow, then sow and tend so that our garden will grow and thrive. As time goes on we must monitor the effects of our watering and fertilizing habits. Most importantly, over the longer term we must periodically ask ourselves if we want to grow more, weed out, or add new types of plants. An unplanned, insufficiently monitored garden will become difficult to manage, consume excessive resources to little effect, produce unintended results, and perhaps wither and die altogether.

Similarly, if a board preoccupies itself with everyday resources and relationship questions to the detriment of monitoring and assessing results, it fails in its governance role and jeopardizes the organization. The board must always keep the big picture in mind, remembering that results may change over time. **BoardSteps** enables a board to do just that: maintain focus on the **results** it wants to see, methodically identify the supporting **relationships** and financial **resources**, and institute mechanisms for monitoring the entire operation.

A board
must stipulate
financial needs,
and then pursue
and allocate
resources in a
manner directly
tied to the
mission and
outcomes.

The Organizational Level

Area of Shared Responsibility

RESULTS: ORGANIZATIONAL LEVEL				
RESULTS			STEP ONE	
RELATIONSHIPS			STEP TWO	
RESOURCES			STEP THREE	
		Board	**SHARED RESPONSIBILITY**	**Management**

In this middle ground, called the area of Shared Responsibility, board capacity interfaces with staff resources to determine the organization's strategic direction.

The **BoardSteps** framework first tackles the macro level of the organization—the area of shared board-management responsibility in Steps One, Two and Three.

In any nonprofit, there are responsibilities that specifically belong to the board and those that are accomplished by management. However, there is a gray area where the best decisions are made with input from both. In this middle ground called the area of **Shared Responsibility**, board capacity interfaces with staff resources to determine the organization's strategic direction. **BoardSteps** recognizes the distinction between this area and the independent areas where the board develops its infrastructure to fulfill its governance role and the executive configures management for operational effectiveness.

In **Shared Responsibility** the global questions are posed about the desired results the organization seeks, then the identification of supporting relationships and needed resources follows. Here, the discussion among directors, and between the board and the executive, allows the partnership to reach informed decisions. The process helps the board set and communicate to management a series of organizational standards, ranging from the organization's reason for existence, to resource allocation priorities, to government reporting timelines.

Realistic organizational results are crafted when management's valuable hands-on insight is balanced by the board's objective perspective. For instance, a nonprofit addresses economic self-sufficiency by placing teens in skill-developing jobs, but the program has recently experienced declining interest. The staff discovers that there is a growing level of illiteracy among the targeted population and teens will not risk humiliation by completing a job application. In a Shared Responsibility discussion, management and the board consider the literacy need as it impacts the employment pool, and in turn, the organizational results.

While the board and the executive share responsibility at the organizational level, it is imperative to reinforce that the board remains *accountable* for all of the organization's activities. No matter what happens or who does it, the board answers for it. Anyone who accepts a directorship should appreciate this distinction between responsibility and accountability, which **BoardSteps** defines as follows:

◆ *Responsibility* lies with an individual or group who directly accomplishes a task or performs a duty.

◆ *Accountability* lies with the individual or group that can and must answer for a given practice, behavior or set of actions, regardless of whether that individual or group actually engages in the behavior or performs the actions.

On the management side, a staff member is *responsible* for certain operations—service delivery, for example. The executive, however, is *accountable* to the board for those operations—their success, their failure, and their consequences. Even though the executive may not actually engage in the operational activity, she must be able to demonstrate to the board that the activity supports pre-determined outcomes without violating ethical organizational standards.

Similarly, each director is *responsible* for fulfilling the board job description, performing individual assignments, participating fully in board meetings, and keeping abreast of trends in the field. Furthermore, as a group of individuals, the board is *responsible* for a variety of tasks

As a collective body, the board is accountable for all organizational actions.

The responsibility-accountability continuum highlights the importance of BoardSteps.

including strategic positioning, performance monitoring and documentation analysis. As a collective, legally constituted entity, however, the board is *accountable* to the public and the government for all organizational actions and decisions, regardless of which board members or staffers are actually *responsible* for taking those actions or making those decisions. As a practical matter, a dependable communication and coordination mechanism must exist between the board and management. Typically, the board chair and the executive develop a formal working relationship to facilitate coordination of shared responsibilities.

The *responsibility-accountability* continuum highlights the importance of **BoardSteps**. It may be understood as the process of establishing structures that minimize the board's risk—and maximize its pride—in being accountable for the actions of individual directors, the executive, the staff, and volunteers.

To institute **BoardSteps**, we first determine the results we want to see at the ***organizational level***. With that understanding in hand, we proceed to the nuts and bolts of the framework.

STEP ONE

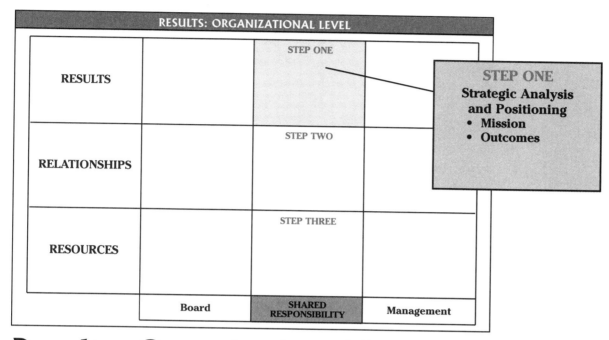

Results: Organizational Level

To paraphrase Supreme Court Justice Potter Stewart, results are difficult to define, but we know them when we see them. At its most basic, a result is the answer to a question. In the case of a nonprofit, the question is, "Why do we do what we do?"

In **BoardSteps**—Step One—the board and executive answer this question through strategic analysis and positioning. Strategic analysis helps the organization realize its place in the world. It provides an objective look at how external and internal trends will influence the nonprofit. With that in mind, it clarifies what the organization wants to achieve, in what context, and for what reasons. These all become codified in the mission statement. Next, the team shifts to strategic positioning, utilizing available information to prioritize feasible outcomes that support the mission, and declaring what the nonprofit will and will not do in pursuit of those outcomes.

The board has an obligation to think beyond the present—to act for the future. The issues most nonprofits address have long-term implications, so it follows that their results cannot be accomplished in the short term. As a consequence, the mission statement and outcome priorities a board authors will shape the organization's decisions and operations for

> The board has an obligation to think beyond the present— to act for the future.

15

years to come, and in most cases well beyond the one-to-three-year dura-tion of a typical board term.

I once assumed a board chair position, and a past leader gave me this sage advice, "So many ideas are germinated in the current term but are not completed for many administrations later. I hope you will expe-rience both the tough work of getting something new off the ground, as well as the exhilaration of seeing something come to fruition... some-thing that someone else initiated." She then recalled the quote, "We can accomplish anything if we don't care who gets the credit." This cap-tures the spirit of governance. An effective board works diligently toward long-term outcomes rather than short-term quick fixes. Past directors should be able to take pride in organizational achievements that result from decisions made during their board term.

Boards and executives often find themselves discussing shorter-term issues involving programs and services before they have fully defined the results those programs and services are meant to support. This is a mistake for three reasons:

◆ It hurts operational efficiency by diluting the organization's focus and weakening its identity and sense of purpose.

◆ It threatens the organization's fiscal health by committing financial resources in an insufficiently coordinated fashion.

◆ It distracts the board from its proper governance function by involving it in internal questions that should be handled by management.

In **BoardSteps**, the board-executive team speaks to the implica-tions of the nonprofit's results. What positive changes will be seen in the community? How will lives be transformed? How will attitudes improve? Keeping these broad questions at the forefront of the discussion differ-entiates between micro-management and governance.

It is possible that a frank exchange will reveal that the organiza-tion should radically alter its mission, merge with another organization, or cease operations altogether. While these choices might be remote, in some situations they may represent the most strategic and accountable options for the board. In any event, putting them on the table helps to guarantee that the discussion proceeds at a sufficiently comprehensive level with no assumptions left unquestioned.

An effective board works diligently toward long-term outcomes.

Tools to Define Organizational Results

I have included five worksheets that will promote discussions of strategic analysis and positioning. By working through them, the board and executive embark on a well-defined path to organizational outcomes. That path proceeds through the following:

◆ Define the mission,

◆ Weigh internal opportunities and challenges,

◆ Weigh external opportunities and challenges,

◆ Articulate the desired outcomes, and

◆ Prioritize those outcomes.

A significant commitment of time is required to develop the content of Step One because it provides the targets that the organization seeks.

The executive's involvement is indispensable to the decisions made here, as she will be charged with translating this direction into an operational plan with programs and services delivered by staff. Collaborating from the outset strengthens the board-executive relationship, boosts management morale, and increases the likelihood that day-to-day operations will in fact support the board's vision for the organization.

As the board moves through the **BoardSteps** framework, it must be aware of where standards are necessary to demonstrate accountability. It will be obvious at certain junctures that the board must say something to guide future organizational decisions. Since it is strongly suggested that the board complete all worksheets before attempting to draft any standards, the board must be confident that its ongoing discussion is well documented.[3] The best way to increase the board's comfort level with this process is to engage a recorder to preserve the dialogue. By waiting and working through the steps, the board will have a much clearer appreciation of the value of the complete Standards Inventory. In addition, the board will have a greater understanding of how it will monitor the inventory as part of its governance role.

[3] The board will find itself discussing some topics in great detail. For example, it may feel that one standard satisfies what it wants to say about financial investing but asset protection requires several standards to document more in-depth comments.

Mission ◆ Worksheet 1A

Achievement of the mission is the ultimate result that the board seeks. A mission statement drives all decision making for the nonprofit and articulates **why** we do **what** we do. It expresses why the organization exists and states the primary purpose or reason for being.

External and Internal Scans ◆ Worksheets 1B and 1C

No organization works in a vacuum. A nonprofit must acknowledge the dynamics inside and outside its walls. By assessing external trends and analyzing internal data, the board can develop outcomes that not only support the mission but also are realistic for the organization and beneficial to the community.

After the External and Internal Scans have been completed, the board may determine that the organizational mission needs to be rewritten. If that is the case, the mission worksheet must be revisited. To facilitate the process, an ad hoc workgroup can be assigned to draft new mission statement options for presentation to the whole board for its consideration.

Organizational Outcomes ◆ Worksheet 1D

While the mission is the ultimate result the nonprofit pursues, the statement itself is too difficult to measure. In order to fulfill its governance function, the board must have some way to monitor organizational performance. So it continues to expand on **why** we do **what** we do, and the mission is underpinned by more detailed results called outcomes.

Using the worksheet, the board and executive write measurable statements that guide organizational and operational decisions in support of the mission. The executive concentrates management activities on meeting the outcomes.

This work presents a challenge for most boards. There is a tendency to elaborate on the mission with phrases like "making a difference," "changing behaviors," and "improving the quality of life." While basic as guiding concepts, these are too vague to quantify and nearly impossible for management to translate into an operational plan. It is essential that the board and executive take the time and address the hard work of translating laudable expressions into measurable statements.

The board continues to expand on <u>why we do what we do</u>, and the mission is underpinned by more detailed results called outcomes.

18

Priorities ◆ Worksheet 1E

Priority setting is one of those items that often falls through the cracks. There is so much to do and never enough revenue with which to do it. Consequently, boards hesitate to set priorities and feel thankful for whatever the nonprofit is able to do. Yet it is precisely because no organization can do everything that the board has a responsibility to decide how resources will be allocated.

BoardSteps wraps human resource costs into the heading of "resources." After all, time is money, and the simple definition allows for clear-cut decisions. By looking at human resources this way, volunteer hours become an added bonus and can be leveraged to maximize operations. With outcomes prioritized, the executive has the direction needed to design the most efficient management infrastructure.

Once our outcomes are defined and prioritized, the area of organizational *relationships* is addressed.

◆ IN REVIEW...

Step One helps your board to:

◆ Establish the mission (Worksheet 1A),

◆ Assess internal and external opportunities and challenges (Worksheets 1B, 1C),

◆ List desired outcomes (Worksheet 1D), and

◆ Prioritize those outcomes (Worksheet 1E).

Each of these exercises builds upon the previous one to create the foundation upon which all future work rests. The prioritized outcomes Worksheet 1E becomes the basis for the relationship and resource work ahead.

STEP TWO

RELATIONSHIPS: ORGANIZATIONAL LEVEL			
RESULTS		**STEP ONE** **Strategic Analysis** **and Positioning** • Mission • Outcomes	
RELATIONSHIPS		STEP TWO	**STEP TWO** **Direct** • **Public Regulator** • **Outcome-driven** **Relationships** **Indirect**
RESOURCES		STEP THREE	
	Board	**SHARED** **RESPONSIBILITY**	**Management**

Relationships: Organizational Level

The nonprofit sector is about people working together on a daily basis to build better communities and improve the human condition. Relationships form the central core of nonprofit service constituting the essence and heartbeat of any organization. The lives of clients, staff, volunteers, funders and board members intersect in a complex web of interactions. Positive relationships produce solid results and help generate financial resources. Negative relationships can dampen spirits, damage image and destroy a hard-earned reputation.

The board is, of course, accountable for the consequences of all organizational relationships, but the board and management best nurture many of these cooperatively. Each board should define organizational relationships based on its particular circumstances. Some very small organizations have no paid staff, and individual directors manage all organizational relationships in the course of filling staff positions on a voluntary basis. On the other end of the spectrum, directors of some larger, well-established nonprofits rarely come into direct contact with the individuals and groups with which the organization interfaces.

No matter where your organization falls in the spectrum, **BoardSteps** can help. In the situation where volunteers perform all tasks, it is very helpful to distinguish between relationships that directors have in their capacity as board members and those they have in their unpaid staff roles. When nonprofits have paid staff, it is crucial that directors value the nature and importance of the various organizational relationships, even if—or especially if—they do not directly participate in them.

A nonprofit has both direct and indirect relationships. Direct relationships are divided into eight basic categories. The first covers the legal relationship every organization is required to have:

1. Public Regulators

The next seven categories cover direct relationships that are significant, and in many cases essential, but that the organization itself chooses and shapes:

2. Funders
3. Clients
4. Volunteers
5. Members
6. Collaborators
7. Third-party Professionals
8. The News Media

Finally, a nonprofit also has a de facto relationship with other individuals or groups touched by its work. These we designate as:

9. Indirect relationships

Relationships form the central core of nonprofit service constituting the essence and heartbeat of any organization.

1. Public Regulators

Any experienced director will likely term the organization's relationship with public regulators as one that is to be taken very seriously. Beyond the forms and the bureaucracy lies the nonprofit's most fundamental relationship. A nonprofit is accountable to the public, and the board-regulator relationship is the means by which accountability is demonstrated.

A public regulator is an organization or agency that represents the public interest in a legal or professional capacity. Public regulators typically share common powers, including:

◆ The power to enforce legal accountability,

◆ The power to set criteria for nonprofit activities, and

◆ The power to impose penalties or mandate remediation for substandard, inappropriate or unlawful nonprofit behavior.

There are two basic types of public regulator: government and accreditor. The federal government grants the tax-exempt status that distinguishes the not-for-profit sector from the for-profit sector. In addition, federal, state and municipal legislatures and agencies approve laws and regulatory procedures that affect the nonprofit at all levels. Accreditors set organizational criteria within specialized fields, evaluate and qualify individual organizations according to the criteria, and periodically review qualified organizations to ensure ongoing compliance. Most of us are familiar with accrediting agencies in the fields of health care and education, but such agencies exist in almost every field of endeavor. Accrediting agencies may be government-affiliated, private but charged with an explicit mandate from government, or entirely private with a mandate from a professional association or some other industry organization.

Relationships with public regulators are unavoidable. They begin when the nonprofit is formed, coming into play during the process of filing initial incorporation papers. While founding directors usually draft the original articles of incorporation, bylaws and tax-exempt applications, most organizations find it most efficient to charge the executive with the subsequent documentation, filing and reporting responsibilities associated with regulatory compliance. The board, for its part, must provide effective oversight of the regulatory process, as the board is the entity that is ultimately accountable to public regulators, and by extension to the general public.

From the global perspective of **BoardSteps,** public regulator relationships are not only necessary but also constructive, since they reinforce public confidence in the nonprofit sector as a whole.

2. Funders

Funders provide the material resources to sustain an organization. Funds may come from public funders (government), private funders (foundations, trusts, businesses, other nonprofits), individual donors, or, typically, a combination of all three. While monetary grants

From the global perspective of BoardSteps, public regulator relationships are not only necessary but also constructive, since they reinforce public confidence in the nonprofit sector as a whole.

and donations comprise the livelihood of a nonprofit, good funder relationships can also generate other gifts in the form of matching funds, donated goods and pro bono professional services. In fact, an abundance of offers for in-kind products and services strongly indicates that the organization is doing a good job of cultivating all sorts of relationships, and that it has a positive image in the community.

Every board member must appreciate that funder relationships are continuous. The all-important grant application or solicitation visit merely marks a single event in an ongoing relationship. Funders must be researched, cultivated, courted, nurtured, kept in the know, and tapped for advice on both organizational direction and other possible funding sources. While nonprofits should avoid constantly chasing new funds to the detriment of daily operational activities, the fact is that both the board and the executive must devote significant time to fostering and maintaining productive, open relationships with funders. The term stewardship, with its connotations of responsible supervision and long-term sustainability, reinforces the seriousness of the connection between a nonprofit and its benefactors.

The division of responsibility for the funder relationship varies considerably with an organization's size, needs and history. In many respects this relationship parallels the one with public regulators: there are many reporting and compliance requirements associated with receiving and spending funds, and the board is accountable for the money flow even though the executive takes responsibility for translating funds into programs, services, staff positions, facilities and equipment. In addition, most organizations require board members to participate in fundraising by soliciting and cultivating funders, and making some kind of annual personal contribution themselves.

3. Clients

A nonprofit fulfills its basic purpose—benefiting communities—by serving target populations and constituencies. While other relationships help the organization pursue its mission, the client relationship is the reason the mission exists in the first place. Clients are the recipients of programs and services and ideally value what is being provided. The board prescribes standards to ensure that this relationship is positive, productive and centered on the safety and well being of the service recipient. The executive then interprets these standards with operational ones.

4. Volunteers

Very few nonprofits can function well—or at all—without volunteers who act as unpaid staff. This relationship is like the funder one given that volunteers must be sustained and nurtured. In addition, volunteers represent a particular combination of right and responsibility. They subordinate themselves to management as they take on a share of responsibility for operational activities; at the same time, they have the option to pick and choose what they do, and to walk away at any time with minimal consequences (for themselves, not the organization). In practice, management will have the lion's share of contact with volunteers, but directors do well to remember the complicated nature of the relationship, the ambiguous position of the volunteer in the organization's hierarchy, and the impact a happy—or unhappy—volunteer can have on the organization's public image.

5. Members

A membership organization—the parent so to speak—both supports and is sustained by its members, whether those members are individuals or affiliated organizations. Member relationships may be understood as a combination of client and funder relationships. The parent serves its members, making them analogous to clients. At the same time, members—particularly affiliated organizations like chapters and branches—act as funders since dues or a portion of locally raised funds are forwarded to the parent organization. This is the most variable of all nonprofit relationships, and it should be assessed and considered closely and carefully so there are no misunderstandings that can hamper the work of each. The question of the relationship between the boards of the parent and the affiliate is by itself sufficient to occupy significant time and examination as the organization moves through this phase of **BoardSteps**.

6. Collaborators

A collaborative relationship begins when representatives from two or more organizations unite to tackle a common concern or accomplish a joint goal. Personal friendships, cross-board membership, or apparent similarities in organizational mission should not motivate the formation of collaborative relationships. These elements can increase the effectiveness of a collaborative enterprise, but strategic considerations must be the motivating force. Collaboration should be undertaken only if it will produce a solid strategic intention: advance outcomes, improve service delivery, conserve revenue, enhance efficiency, influence public policy, increase fundraising, and so on.

7. Third-party Professionals

Often a nonprofit will require the services of a professional consultant for a particular project, initiative or problem. Management frequently will retain the services of print and Web designers, trainer-facilitators, and management consultants. By the same token, the board engages auditors, accountants, attorneys, and experts in the nonprofit's field of endeavor, to assist in compliance, financial management, education and strategic thinking. Determining the organization's need for third-party professionals goes hand-in-hand with assessing the organization's opportunities and challenges.

8. The News Media

The prospect of interacting with the news media strikes fear in the heart of many a director: after all, nonprofit boards seem to garner media coverage only when allegations of malfeasance come to light. In recent years, governance controversies at prominent national nonprofits have brought increased media attention to board activities, which has only heightened anxiety about the media in the nonprofit sector.

A moment of reflection, however, yields a different opinion. Most nonprofits enjoy good relations with the media, particularly local media, on a regular basis. The bulk of attention to nonprofits consists of human-interest stories on organizational initiatives, spotlight pieces on upcoming events, profiles of individual staff members or clients, and listings of service schedules or operating hours. Through these run-of-the-mill interactions with the news media, a nonprofit increases public awareness of itself and its mission, and creates community goodwill—all of which enhance its ability to cultivate other types of relationships.

Management usually bears responsibility for sustaining these everyday media relationships. By virtue of the leadership position, the executive or board chair serve as spokesperson unless it is determined to be more advantageous for an individual director to be available for public comment. This is particularly valuable in the case of a director

Determining the organization's need for third-party professionals goes hand-in-hand with assessing the organization's opportunities and challenges.

whose professional skills complement the nonprofit's mission, such as a doctor for a drug treatment program or a nutritionist for a food co-op. This expert can highlight the work of the nonprofit within the context of the greater issue.

9. Indirect Relationships

Direct relationships are more familiar than indirect ones, and they rightly take up more board and staff time. Yet a nonprofit ignores indirect relationships at its own peril. Take into consideration the direct relationship with the news media, which is also a conduit for a larger, indirect relationship with the general public. After all, it is the nonprofit's indirect relationship with the public, not its direct relationship with the media that benefits or suffers depending on what kind of news coverage the organization garners.

Individuals who are touched in a peripheral way by the organization's activities constitute indirect relationships. They are difficult to pinpoint and control, and so a board should not become preoccupied with trying to micromanage them. An organization should, however, remain cognizant of the public impact of its activities and positions. For example, a nonprofit providing sterile syringe exchange for drug users will need to pay very close attention to the effect its operations have on the neighborhood in which it is located. It must proactively get the word out about the health safety standards that guide its work. If it does not design its client outreach materials with the understanding that members of the general public will also end up reading them, it will soon find itself besieged by criticism or even fighting for its survival.

Tools to Define
Organizational Relationships

For the work of Step Two, the board uses three worksheets for identifying and sustaining key relationships. By discussing and working through them, the board and executive make certain that the organization's interactions support results.

Legal Relationships: Public Regulators ◆ Worksheet 2A

The organization must take stock of its numerous relationships with public regulators. The time commitment required to document, initiate and sustain these may seem daunting, but a full assessment now will assist greatly in future strategic and tactical planning. It will also reduce the likelihood that staff will have to be pulled away from other, more immediate tasks in order to help with compliance issues at the eleventh hour.

Legal Compliance Checklist and Schedule ◆ Worksheet 2B

Once a list of regulators has been compiled, the board must create a comprehensive legal compliance checklist and schedule. Compliance demands a multi-dimensional approach. It must be understood and coordinated in regard to each type of regulator: To begin, all steps of incorporating the nonprofit in its home state must be outlined in a way that makes sense. At the same time, however, each part of the compliance process must be delineated in its own right, so that responsibility may be assigned within the organization. Who will keep track of the reporting schedule and who will be responsible for preparing and reviewing which documents? Then, compliance items must be coordinated with each other: Application for state-level incorporation, for instance, must be synchronized with application for federal tax-exempt status to avoid unnecessary bureaucratic delays.

While all aspects of the **BoardSteps** process require thoughtful, focused deliberation, the legal compliance checklist is the most complex of the worksheets. I suggest that your board engage an attorney with nonprofit experience to help develop this tool. Using an outside professional with no ties to your organization provides the opportunity to:

◆ Obtain accurate, up-to-date advice,

◆ Educate the board about the legal aspects of its job, and

◆ Have directors' questions answered by an unbiased party.

Once the checklist has been developed, the board must review it on a regular basis to ensure it remains complete and accurate in the face of inevitable changes in laws and regulations over time.

Note that while some of these legal relationships consist solely of filing documents, others do not. Particularly on the local and state levels, constructive relationships with public regulators may include face-to-face

> Once a list of regulators has been compiled, the board must create a comprehensive legal compliance checklist and schedule.

meetings, and periodic informal conversations about trends in government and the sector. Moreover, the organization may choose to enhance its image, reinforce its ethical standards, or increase its attractiveness to possible funders, by voluntarily seeking the quasi-regulatory approval of additional accreditors or "watchdog" groups.

Outcome-driven Organizational Relationships
◆ **Worksheet 2C**

The nonprofit's relationship with public regulators is mandated. In contrast, its results determine the nature and scope of its other relationships (funders,[4] clients, volunteers, members, collaborators, third-party professionals, the news media, and indirect ones).

Now, the work resumes with the prioritized outcomes formulated in Step One (Worksheet 1E) and proceeds on to link targeted relationships with organizational results. This worksheet should be copied and completed for each outcome. Any number of relationships may come into play, and consequently, some relationships may appear several times.

For each outcome:

◆ Identify the people or organization linkage,

◆ Assign responsibility for cultivating the relationship,

◆ Define the shared responsibility,

◆ State clearly why the relationship is needed,

◆ Assign coordination of responsibilities, and

◆ Document the need for standards for maintaining and evaluating the relationship.

When the worksheets have been completed, the relationships appearing for multiple outcomes should be noted. The value of the executive's involvement cannot be underestimated here, as she will be charged with developing and maintaining most of the identified relationships, and with allocating resources accordingly. When the executive has input into the linkage-mapping process, she has a better understanding about how to sustain these critical relationships.

[4] In this step, only the need for a funder is noted. The particular funder is identified later in Step Three.

Coordination Responsibility

It is easy to say that the best decisions result from the board-management interactions in the Shared Responsibility steps but there is always the potential for weakness at this interface. The board must guard against a blurring of the lines about **who is responsible for what.**

In **BoardSteps** there is a practical need for coordination in the Shared Responsibility steps. The act of coordinating is in itself a task that has to be assigned to someone. The board must maintain an awareness of this assignment since success can vary greatly depending on the commitment of the leadership of the board or the staff. By the very nature of their jobs, the board chair and executive bear this responsibility. They must communicate with each other, confirm assignments and monitor for completion. The board as a collective body holds each accountable for the coordination function.

◆ IN REVIEW...

Step Two helps your board to:

◆ Identify public regulators for your organization (Worksheet 2A),

◆ Develop a legal compliance checklist and schedule (Worksheet 2B), and

◆ Identify relationships based on each prioritized outcome (Worksheet 2C).

The checklist is monitored on the board's regular agenda and the official minutes document compliance. This constitutes a significant part of the governance demand to demonstrate accountability. Linking prioritized outcomes and relationships allows the board-executive team to define what interaction is needed, why, and when it should happen. In order for this hard work to pay off, however, the organization must obtain and manage the resources that are to be allocated. This is the focus of Step Three.

STEP THREE

RESOURCES: ORGANIZATIONAL LEVEL			
RESULTS		**STEP ONE** Strategic Analysis and Positioning • Mission • Outcomes	
RELATIONSHIPS		**STEP TWO** Direct • Public Regulators • Outcome-driven Relationships Indirect	
RESOURCES		**STEP THREE**	
	Board	**SHARED RESPONSIBILITY**	**Management**

STEP THREE

Financial Analysis
Fund Development
• **Outcome-driven**
Resources

Resources: Organizational Level

Say the word "board" to someone familiar with nonprofits, and immediately fundraising comes to mind. If an organization's mission and relationships form its heart and soul, then monetary capital is its lifeblood. It is safe to say that, over the years, financial matters have deprived nonprofit leadership of more good nights of sleep than all other matters combined.

Yet the resource step is the last organizational level component covered in the framework, not the first. We discussed the reason for this in the Introduction: without sound strategic planning resulting in the prioritization of outcomes and relationships, a nonprofit cannot pursue or make use of resources in a productive manner.

Furthermore, fundraising itself is only half the resources story. In order to govern fully and correctly, the board needs to involve itself in two main tasks: **financial analysis** and **fund development**. Consistent with the **BoardSteps** philosophy, financial management and reporting systems must be put into place before the organization engages in serious fundraising.

Without sound strategic planning resulting in the prioritization of outcomes and relationships, a nonprofit cannot pursue or make use of resources in a productive manner.

Financial Analysis

The board bears the responsibility of financial analysis to demonstrate stewardship and accountability. But, before it can analyze anything, it needs to determine the appropriate financial management system that provides the necessary details. Financial management has always been seen as a largely technical matter, and the introduction of relatively inexpensive computerized financial accounting software in the last two decades has only reinforced that perception.

While financial management certainly involves technical minutiae, it is much more than that. It reaches into the center of the organization's structure. In order to govern responsibly, the board must examine the organization's finances. Before it does that, however, it must work with the executive to determine the nature, extent and presentation of the financial data itself. How many internal funds will the organization use to organize the money it raises? How should the accounting system be organized? What standards are there for limiting administrative overhead? How much expense-tracking detail is necessary, without overtaxing staff? When should the fiscal year begin and end? These are some of the many questions a board and executive should ask as they consider the best way to manage and protect monetary assets.

In planning the organization's financial management system, the board functions much like a prospective homeowner, and the executive like a builder. The homeowner describes what the house will look like, and the functions the house must accommodate. The builder's job is to point out potential difficulties, suggest pragmatic changes and improvements, and then create the actual structure according to the agreed-upon plan. Likewise, the board articulates a financial management structure that will allow it to oversee use of resources, and the executive implements sound systems that produce the necessary documentation for the board (and auditors) to examine.

Before a house is built, an architect is usually retained to translate the homeowner's vision into a formal blueprint in order to make sure that everyone involved is working from the same foundation. By the same token, **BoardSteps** strongly recommends that all boards—particularly boards of small or young organizations—retain a third party professional to provide guidance on the design and presentation of the financials.

Once the financial structure has been determined and management has instituted the necessary systems, the board must engage in ongoing

The board articulates a financial management structure that will allow it to oversee use of resources.

financial analysis. This is the responsibility of the entire board. Some directors mistakenly believe that fiscal liability can be off-loaded to the board treasurer or an auditor. This could not be further from the truth. The treasurer works with the executive to present financial information, but it is the board as a whole that is responsible for analyzing the information and mandating any necessary changes. Likewise, an auditor only ensures that the organization's finances are legally in order and that its financial accounting systems allow it to comply with Generally Accepted Accounting Practices (GAAP). All other aspects of financial management, both grand and small, fall in the board camp.

Because final accountability for the nonprofit's assets falls squarely on the board, each director is legally and ethically bound to be aware of, and participate fully in, decision-making concerning organizational finances. For this reason, directors need to be educated—by the board treasurer, the executive, or a third party professional—about the system that management uses.[5] Each director must know the fiscal standards, understand the financial systems, and review the applicable documents— no exceptions! Without a common understanding, the board's debates about financial priorities get bogged down in management issues.

As is the case with organizational relationships, organizational finances should be analyzed according to Results: Are we managing our resources in a way that supports our desired outcomes?

Like every other aspect of nonprofit governance covered thus far, accurate financial analysis requires a framework of shared responsibility and clear standards.

Fund Development

Nonprofits spend an inordinate amount of time pursuing funding since money is the fuel that keeps programs running and organizations afloat. The most successful ones utilize a fund development plan to coordinate fundraising activities that may include grant applications, special events, annual giving programs, capital campaigns, and a host of other revenue-producing endeavors. Naturally, the board helps complete the plan by obtaining funds, using its contacts and making its own contributions.

Fundraising operations vary tremendously in design and scope. Some nonprofits have large development divisions, while others have none at all. No matter how large or small the fundraising operation, it is the board that must make certain the organization has sufficient financial

[5] Board training regarding organizational financial systems is mandatory in annual orientation. Incoming directors must have a clear understanding of how the board monitors financials.

resources to operate. In this respect, fund development is quite different from the determination of outcomes. An organization that fails to achieve, say, two out of its ten desired outcomes may still be considered successful. In such a bind, the board and executive may decide to rearrange priorities to promote progress on the two elusive outcomes. If, however, an organization fails to raise 20 percent of the budget needed to sustain programs to which it has already committed itself, the consequences may be dire. Already-procured funds may have to be returned to a funder if the organization does not have enough money to carry out the programs for which the funds were raised. In short, for many small- to medium-sized nonprofits, a 20 percent funding shortfall can result in the doors being shut for good.

The board's participation in fundraising is defined by the fund development plan. Management provides the necessary administrative support to directors to achieve monetary targets. Participation may include writing letters, making presentations to funders, brokering meetings with prospects, or calling on individuals. It is a rare nonprofit that cannot benefit from fundraising assistance by the board. When dealing with individual donors in particular, a board member may seem more convincing than staff, volunteers, or even the executive depending on circumstances. No matter who seeks the gifts, however, the board has ultimate accountability for ensuring that the organization raises funds to carry out its programs and achieve the desired results.

In addition, the board sets the tone by making individual annual contributions, actively participating in fundraising campaigns, and attending events that raise money or strengthen relationships with existing and prospective funders. There may be circumstances in which requiring every director to make an annual gift is unwise or infeasible, but such situations are much rarer than the conventional wisdom would have us believe.

Generally speaking, every board member should contribute to the organization on an annual basis. Even if the minimum contribution is set at $5, having 100% participation each year is absolutely imperative if the nonprofit intends to obtain any funds from private foundations and individual donors. If directors don't support the organization in some financial way, why should anyone else? Leading by example in fund development is a critical part of the board's role.

Director contributions are therefore a relatively uncomplicated matter. A standard in this area declares the expectation, sets a minimum

> **Leading by example in fund development is a critical part of the board's role.**

amount, and may set a second, higher preferred amount. In addition, the board may wish to set an aggregate standard. When applied in combination with a modest individual standard, it can motivate directors with sufficient means and desire to give more, while avoiding discomfort for others. Finally, the board may wish to stipulate expectations on in-kind contributions of time, professional services, or equipment.

It is worth noting that a growing number of nonprofits are investigating new funding methods to reduce their dependency on grants and gifts. The social entrepreneurial movement has stimulated new thinking about earned income. For-profit subsidiaries, sponsorships and affinity partnerships represent some of the non-traditional vehicles to enhance organizational self-sufficiency. Every board should keep abreast of these developments and explore the options if desired. However, these approaches are not quick fixes, and it is advisable that young nonprofits solidify the fundamentals before branching out into these new territories.

Tools to Identify and Manage Organizational Resources

Financial Analysis ◆ Worksheet 3A

The board must understand its organization's financial reporting system and have confidence that the financial statements provide accurate and timely information to inform its decisions. Therefore, each nonprofit will approach this from its particular position. Some organizations will begin by hiring a professional to help with the design of its systems. Others will be satisfied with the current presentation of the financials. Training may be necessary for some boards. Whatever the starting point, the board and executive must work together to ensure that all directors are clear about how to analyze financial data.

Once the board has addressed financial analysis, it moves on to identify the categories of standards that will guide resource decisions. This requires a facilitated discussion focusing on responsible supervision. Usually, a lengthy debate will result that generates many concerns of directors and these must be recorded for the standards-writing assignment. Standards categories may include, but not be limited to: financial planning, budgeting, conditions, asset protection and investments.

This worksheet offers some initial discussion points to determine the pulse of the board regarding the finances. Since a workgroup will be appointed to draft standards after the completion of the six steps of Section 2, the board may delegate this work to the writing team.

Outcome-driven Funder Identification ◆ Worksheet 3B

Just as with relationships, all resource decisions must be tied to organizational outcomes. Step Three helps your organization target probable funders. This worksheet should be copied and completed for each outcome.

The fundamental resource question is what funder might support the kind of work necessary to achieve a result. Outlining specific responsibilities regarding contact or cultivation is fundamental to securing resources. Beyond generating the content of this worksheet, it is management's responsibility to determine revenue needs and present them to the board in the form of a budget. Now we've come full circle since the board can confidently analyze the budget in light of prioritized outcomes and with a clear understanding of the financial management system and pre-determined standards.

◆ IN REVIEW...

Step Three helps your board to:

◆ Establish the financial management and reporting systems it will use for monitoring (Worksheet 3A), and

◆ Identify potential funders for each prioritized outcome (Worksheet 3B).

Agreement has been reached on the financial management system that provides the board with data it needs to exercise governance oversight. Outcomes are matched with prospects for funding.

This completes the Organizational Level: Shared Responsibility work of Steps One, Two and Three.

The Organizational Level Shared Responsibility: Recap

RESULTS = RELATIONSHIPS + RESOURCES: ORGANIZATIONAL LEVEL			
RESULTS		**STEP ONE** **Strategic Analysis and Positioning** • Mission • Outcomes	
RELATIONSHIPS		**STEP TWO** Direct • Public Regulators • Outcome-driven Relationships Indirect	
RESOURCES		**STEP THREE** **Financial Analysis** **Fund Development** • Outcome-driven Resources	
	Board	SHARED RESPONSIBILITY	Management

At this point we have completed the organizational level work in the Shared Responsibility steps. The leadership has shaped the non-profit's external face by defining its human interactions and focusing its public efforts.

To summarize, the board-executive partnership:

◆ Analyzed available information to craft the mission and prioritize outcomes,

◆ Identified legal and outcome-related relationships,

◆ Addressed a financial management structure to oversee resources and a fund development plan tied to organizational outcomes.

Indeed, each individual step, and all the steps in the aggregate, clarify who is responsible for what, and to what degree. None of the worksheets—or the tasks that follow—can be accomplished without shared board-management responsibility within a context of ultimate board accountability.

We now turn our attention to the board and how it will organize to support the work of the Shared Responsibility area.

The Board Level

	RESULTS = RELATIONSHIPS + RESOURCES: BOARD LEVEL		
RESULTS	STEP FOUR	STEP ONE	
RELATIONSHIPS	STEP FIVE	STEP TWO	
RESOURCES	STEP SIX	STEP THREE	
	Board	**SHARED RESPONSIBILITY**	**Management**

As stated earlier, the **BoardSteps** process is divided into two distinct levels:

◆ The **organizational level**, in which the board and the executive collaborate to define desirable and attainable results, and develop an appropriate division of labor and responsibility; and

◆ The **board level**, in which the board establishes the proper infrastructure, and working relationships necessary for it to act responsibly and ultimately demonstrate accountability.

As with the orchestra comparison, these two levels distinguish between the performance and the preparation that makes it a success. The symphony audience benefits from the behind-the-scenes practice, discipline and dedication of the musicians; the nonprofit's community gains from the participation of committed and knowledgeable board members.

Steps Four, Five and Six allow the board to concentrate on how it will organize to be an effective player in the board-management equation. At this point, directors focus inward to build the support system that underpins and facilitates their actions to see that organizational results are accomplished. Here, unlike in the shared responsibility area,

> **Steps Four, Five and Six allow the board to concentrate on how it will organize to be an effective player in the board-management equation.**

tasks and relationships belong expressly to the board and/or individual board members.

The board level work is different from anything we have done so far. We are creating the infrastructure that will support future board work. This requires us to take a varied approach, as each step will generate different kinds of content regarding what the board has to say about its own results, relationships and resources. Also, educational governance material is interspersed throughout the text. Hopefully, it will help the board reach the best decisions about its internal design.

At the organizational level, we determined that standards would be written after the completion of all the worksheets. But at the board level, we take our first look at how standards will be organized. The board will identify the broad categories or headings it wants to use in its Standards Inventory, then it will further expand on each category. For example, Board Operations umbrellas a list of standards that include board meetings, agendas, calendar, retreats, etc. Eventually, the Standards Inventory and the board's discussion record will form the basis for the actual standards writing exercise.

In the case where a nonprofit already has policies in place that the board believes are adequate to guide its work, **BoardSteps** encourages a review of the content, then a modification of the policies[6] to fit the standards inventory format. Current directors draw on individual perspective and personal experience to rewrite old standards to strengthen the board's infrastructure. Reflection, creativity and strategic thinking add to the mix. This new conversation is invaluable as it builds trust and takes advantage of the wealth of wisdom of board members.

In addition, state statutes may dictate that some of the suggested standards be included in bylaws. For clarity and convenience, the board might choose to cross-reference the standard or to duplicate it in the inventory, so it can be seen as part of the whole. In that way, when changes become necessary—amendments, updates, additions or deletions—it makes sense to do so within the context of the entire inventory.

[6] As stated in A Note on Terminology, the terms *policy* and *standard* are interchangeable.

STEP FOUR

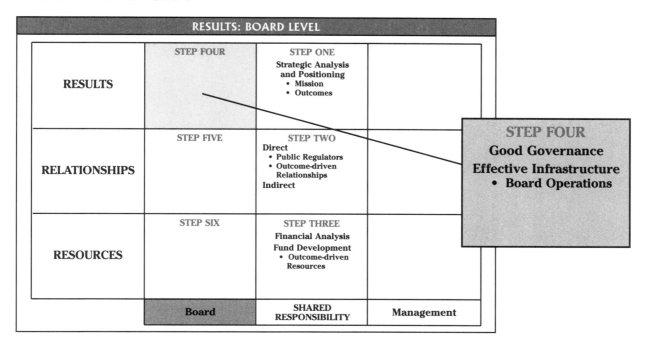

Results: Board Level

Just as the organization exists to benefit the community, the board exists to make certain the nonprofit runs properly. *It exists to govern.* This simple phrase captures what **BoardSteps** believes is the board's sole reason for being. Step Four emphasizes that every board—no exception—must establish **Good Governance** as the primary result it seeks.

Directors begin by writing a <u>Statement of Commitment</u>[7]—an articulation of their pledge to practice good governance, to add value to the organization, and to demonstrate accountability to the public. The discussion about what to include in this statement is incredibly constructive because it concentrates the board's attention and energy on defining the unique role it plays in the life of the nonprofit. A word of caution: Avoid the tendency to call this a board mission statement because it will surely cause confusion for everyone involved.

The <u>Statement</u> will vary with the particular situation of each board. Some examples of content are noted in the following box.

[7] The Statement of Commitment should be shared with all board candidates before an invitation is extended for board service. Then an incoming director joins the board with a full appreciation of what is expected in terms of commitment, responsibility and ultimate accountability.

The Board of Directors of XYZ Center will:

Practice the highest level of governance at our board table to demonstrate accountability to the public and to add value to the organization.

Adopt and monitor a comprehensive inventory of standards that outline our own results, relationships and resources to support the organizational level standards.

Provide annual governance training for the current board and incoming directors.

Value differences of opinion and perspectives to enrich our debates toward better decisions.

Ask each director to sign this good governance pledge since it requires additional time and, more than likely, personal resources for individual education.

> **A Statement of Commitment gives directors (both existing and prospective) and management a sense of the collective personality of the board.**

A <u>Statement of Commitment</u> gives directors (both existing and prospective) and management a sense of the collective personality of the board. The process of thinking through what it means to make this commitment is in itself a benefit to a board's cohesiveness and purpose. In personalizing the statement, the board talks about how it will model ethical behavior and fulfill responsibilities. In addition, directors are compelled to examine their relationships with and respect for each other.

As part of the <u>Statement</u>, **BoardSteps** recommends a second board result—the development of an effective infrastructure. While the fine points of this infrastructure will be addressed in later worksheets, here the board acknowledges that laying this groundwork is central to the practice of good governance.

The sample inventory that follows gives us the first glimpse of how the standards inventory might look. It provides a complete picture—presenting broad categories of standards as they relate to results, relationships and resources—both board and organizational. While **BoardSteps** suggests these categories, some boards will amend the content in light of their specific situations. Even though the work of Steps Five and Six have not been addressed yet, it is recognized here as part of the greater concept. Tying the levels together emphasizes how clear-cut it can be to regularly monitor a category of standards as part of the board agenda.

Some circumstances require the board to direct its attention to additional results. If this is the case, it must be certain that the result meets the internal parameters and does not more appropriately belong in the shared responsibility area. As with outcomes, when internal results are added, there will be a need to prioritize, particularly if the board is small or inexperienced, or if the list gets too long.

Sample STANDARDS INVENTORY

1. Results: Organizational Level

A. Implementation of **BoardSteps**
B. Recognition of Shared Responsibility Area
C. Strategic Analysis and Positioning
D. Mission
E. Prioritized Outcomes

2. Relationships: Organizational Level

A. Direct Relationships
   - Public Regulators
B. Outcome-driven Relationships
C. Indirect Relationships

3. Resources: Organizational Level

A. Financial Analysis
   - Financial Management Systems
B. Fund Development
   - Outcome-driven Resources

4. Results: Board Level

A. Good Governance
B. Effective Infrastructure
   - Board Operations

5. Relationships: Board Level

A. Board-Executive Link
B. Board-Director
   - Board Structure
   - Board Performance
   - Individual Director Performance
C. Director-Prospective/New Director
   - Board Development

6. Resources: Board Level

A. Cost of Good Governance
B. Identification of Needed Resources

Tools to Define Board Results

Statement of Commitment ◆ Worksheet 4A

The <u>Statement</u> should be the board's personal expression of commitment, distinctiveness, values and any other components it wishes to include.

External Scan ◆ Worksheet 4B

Just like the nonprofit, the board functions in the real world. It must examine trends outside the boardroom that may influence job performance. To be clear, the external scan takes into account situations in both the organization and greater world. By assessing and analyzing trends, the board can proactively tackle the challenges and capitalize on the opportunities that influence its ability to practice good governance.

Internal Scan ◆ Worksheet 4C

With the internal scanning worksheet, all directors examine what is happening within the board and each must agree to an open and honest conversation. Listing strengths is a gratifying exercise and, rightfully so. However, dancing around difficult topics, such as destructive behavior and counterproductive practices, will not lead to any helpful changes. The content that is generated here should improve board performance, so by necessity, it must address barriers to that end.

The board uses these scanning worksheets to uncover what might affect its work around the board table. The content will impact internal results, relationships and resources and must be considered in each step.

Board Operations Standards ◆ Worksheet 4D

At this point, we begin developing inventories under the broad category headings. Board Operations standards are the first ones to be addressed and they will facilitate the work of the collective body. The board amends or adds to the inventory and records specific comments for the workgroup that will actually draft the standards.

◆ IN REVIEW...

Step Four helps your board to:

◆ Establish a <u>Statement of Commitment</u> to Good Governance and an Effective Infrastructure (Worksheet 4A),

◆ Assess its internal and external opportunities and challenges (Worksheets 4B, 4C), and

◆ Identify the Board Operations Standards Inventory (Worksheet 4D).

The board concentrates on organizing to become a competent part of the board-management equation. In its collective voice, it commits to the creation of an infrastructure that underpins its practice of good governance. The organization's Standards Inventory begins to be developed.

STEP FIVE

STEP FIVE
Board – Executive Link
Board – Director
• Structure
• Performance
Board – Prospective/
New Director
• Board Development

RELATIONSHIPS: BOARD LEVEL			
RESULTS	**STEP FOUR** Good Governance Effective Infrastructure • Board Operations	**STEP ONE** Strategic Analysis and Positioning • Mission • Outcomes	
RELATIONSHIPS	**STEP FIVE**	**STEP TWO** Direct • Public Regulators • Outcome-driven Relationships Indirect	
RESOURCES	**STEP SIX**	**STEP THREE** Financial Analysis Fund Development • Outcome-driven Resources	
	Board	**SHARED RESPONSIBILITY**	**Management**

Relationships: Board Level

Like the organization itself, the board cannot achieve results without tapping into an intricate network of relationships. First, it is useful to think of the board as an entity unto itself. Directors meld into the collective body that holds the power of the corporation and meets in formal session to make organizational decisions.

In its single voice the board conveys certain conditions regarding the board—executive and executive—director relationships. Next, it sorts out the board—director relationships under the broad categories of structure and performance. Finally, board—prospective/new director relationships encompass board development standards. For most boards, the relationships are the same. However, where this may vary, the relationship in question must meet the test of an internal, board level one and not one that belongs in the Shared Responsibility steps.

The difference between responsibility and accountability was set forth earlier in the organizational level but it bears repeating again as it applies to the various relationships of the board and the individual director. Anyone who accepts a directorship should appreciate this distinction between responsibility and accountability, which is defined as follows:

◆ *Responsibility* lies with an individual or group who directly accomplishes a task or performs a duty.

◆ *Accountability* lies with the individual or group that can and must answer for a given practice, behavior or set of actions, regardless of whether that individual or group actually engages in the behavior or performs the actions.

Each director is *responsible* for fulfilling the board job description, performing individual assignments, participating fully in board meetings, and keeping abreast of trends in the field. Furthermore, as a group of individuals, the board is *responsible* for a variety of tasks including strategic positioning, performance monitoring and documentation analysis. As a collective, legally constituted entity, however, the board is *accountable* to the public and the government for all organizational actions and decisions, regardless of which board members or staffers are actually *responsible* for taking those actions or making those decisions.

Board-Executive Relationship

The board, as a whole, engages, supports, evaluates, and when necessary, dismisses and replaces the executive. Wise directors acknowledge that the management function is complex and seek the most qualified candidate for the position. In the interviewing and selection process, a search workgroup looks for the applicant with the strongest credentials and skills to benefit the organization. Keeping this in mind, after employment, the board should not hamper the talent it was so eager to hire by micromanaging her every move.

The link between the board and the executive is critical to organizational success. In hiring an executive, the board makes a conscious decision to delegate certain responsibilities to its one employee who serves as its connection to the rest of the staff. Clear standards must be in place around this fundamental governing interface. Agreed-to job descriptions, approved channels of communication, and pre-determined performance criteria go a long way in forging a strong partnership and building trust.

BoardSteps ties the executive's performance to that of the organization. By monitoring standards generated in the Shared Responsibility steps, the board can determine if management is effectively directing its efforts toward results and acting within the legal and ethical parameters set forth in relationships and resources. Evaluation is straightforward since the board has already said what it expects to happen over a certain period of time.

The link between the board and the executive is critical to organizational success.

45

The increasing focus on accountability in the sector makes this relationship even more significant. The board that grasps its own job will work well with a strong executive and it will have a higher level of comfort with her ability to manage the nonprofit.

A Word About Directors Performing Management Tasks

Many times directors volunteer to perform management tasks when the nonprofit cannot afford to hire all the staff it needs. When this happens, it must be understood that this is not part of the board function. Boards do not implement programs but directors who serve in an unpaid staff capacity may find themselves doing so. A good illustration is when a board member agrees to manage a temporary project. More than likely, a staff member will oversee the work and the executive will be accountable to the board for its completion. In this circumstance, the director now appropriately reports to staff, and it should be obvious that the perception of any governing status or power is inaccurate. When the rules change it becomes complicated for all involved parties, so both the board and director must make it clear that this is a newly configured relationship. Otherwise, everything the director says to staff will be taken as a mandate rather than a suggestion—direction rather than advice—and there will be a great deal of unproductive maneuvering.

In the event an organization has no paid staff, it goes without saying that directors will do whatever job they must to keep the nonprofit afloat. However, it is still advantageous for the board to distinguish between a director performing a management versus a governance task. Then at a future date when staff might be hired, the management activities are already outlined and can be delegated in a more organized way.

Board-Director Relationship

The categories of structure and performance fall under the board—director relationship. The whole board measures individual performance and it must enforce the standards it has formulated. It is well documented that the morale of any group can be dramatically swayed by the positive or negative actions of one member. This certainly holds true for a nonprofit board. While it has the opportunity to value and applaud exceptional individual service, it is also obligated to enforce its own rules of conduct when they are being violated. It goes without saying that board action begins with one or two directors exercising their responsibility, triggering the consciousness of the whole board.

> **Boards do not implement programs but directors who serve in an unpaid staff capacity may find themselves doing so.**

Good examples are included in a board's conflict of interest and attendance standards:

◆ Conflict of Interest
   1. Directors must conduct themselves in such a way as to avoid any conflict of interest with respect to their governing responsibilities.
   2. Any conflict will be disclosed to the board.
   3. The involved director will not vote, use personal influence, or be counted in the meeting's quorum. The meeting minutes will document this situation.

◆ Attendance
   Directors will:
   1. Attend all board meetings.
   2. Arrive prepared to fully participate in board discussions and decisions.
   3. Recognize responsibility for business conducted and any decisions made at board meetings they are unable to attend.

Each director must meet legal performance standards of conduct and understand what behavior demonstrates compliance.

Measurement and monitoring are pre-determined without the biases of personalities. When the standard is applied objectively to all directors it becomes apparent who is in violation. The board cannot be diverted from its responsibility even when the director is a well-meaning person. Board and individual commitment are clearly articulated and respected.

BoardSteps also includes in the board-director heading the various structural relationships that facilitate the work of the group: board-chair, board-workgroups, and board-officers.

Legal Standards of Conduct and the Individual Director

Each director must meet legal performance standards of conduct and understand what behavior demonstrates compliance.

The Guidebook for Directors of Nonprofit Corporations, published by the American Bar Association, states that "the individual director is subject to two primary obligations: a Duty of Care and a Duty of Loyalty. Duty of Care calls upon a director to participate in the decisions of the board and to be informed as to data relevant to such decisions. Duty of Loyalty requires that a director be informed and exercise independent judgment."

Briefly, directors are responsible for all actions taken at board meetings, even if they were not present. In addition, loyalty to the organization must come before personal gain. Standards regarding possible conflicts of interest and appearances of impropriety are imperative in today's climate of increased litigation.

BoardSteps emphasizes that the board speaks in a single voice. In order to reach that point, each director is duty-bound to be prepared, to actively participate, and exercise independent judgment in making any decision. Once a board decision is made it is declared in a unified expression.

The independent sector might take notice of another duty included in *The Director's Handbook: A Guide for Directors of Privately Held Corporations*. The Duty of Attention stresses attendance at and preparation for meetings. Unfortunately, some nonprofit directors do not feel the urgency to attend or arrive prepared to discharge their duties. The increased scrutiny of board behavior in all sectors reinforces the need for more professionalism at the governing table.

Board-Prospective/New Director Relationship

The board must perpetuate itself, and it does this in a planned manner. Board development is a vital component of the governance role. Recruitment, nomination, election, and orientation combined with mentoring and education is a year-round job for a board workgroup.

By looking at the organization's strategic direction, a board development workgroup can identify skills it wants incoming directors to bring. It should seek candidates who are not only committed to the mission but whose knowledge base will help inform upcoming board decisions. With that information, current directors can cultivate candidates and introduce them to the organization in a thoughtful way. This long-range approach also allows time for potential board members to serve in workgroups or volunteer in some capacity to become more familiar with the nonprofit's work.

Serving as a steward of the public trust is serious business. To build a board or keep one strong, the board development workgroup must be honest with any candidate about expectations and realities. No one wants to hear information after the fact that might have influenced the decision to join the board. In turn, the prospective director must weigh interest, time and financial demands, and be comfortable with the governance and management systems in use.

"Duty of Loyalty requires that a director be informed and exercise independent judgment."

Tools to Define Board Relationships

The board agrees on the categories of standards regarding its relationships. An inventory is developed under each heading and expanded until directors are satisfied that they have addressed everything they wish to say.

Categories of Relationships Standards

Board-Executive ◆ Worksheet 5A

- Link

Board-Director ◆ Worksheet 5B

- Board Structure
- Board Performance
- Individual Director Performance

Board-Prospective/New Director ◆ Worksheet 5C

- Board Development

Standards for this section may sound very familiar and many boards have addressed these internal relationships in one form or another. However, the board should review the content of any existing policies to determine if they incorporate the board's current thinking, then write new standards in the suggested **BoardSteps** format.

◆ IN REVIEW...

Step Five helps your board to:

◆ Identify its internal relationships,

◆ Establish the broad categories of standards, and

◆ Develop Board-Executive Link, Board Structure, Performance, and Development Standards Inventories (Worksheets 5A, 5B, 5C).

Board relationships—board-executive, board-director, board-prospective/new director—set the stage for the work of the governing body.

STEP SIX

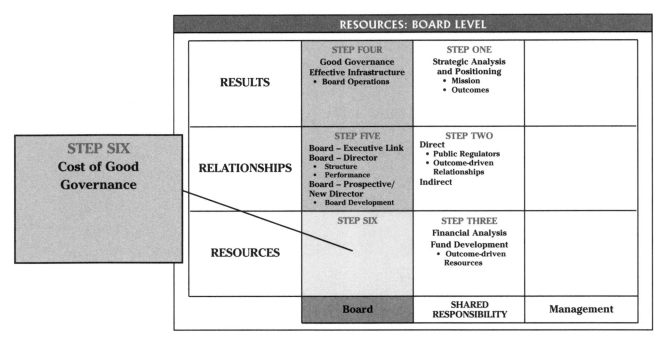

RESOURCES: BOARD LEVEL			
RESULTS	**STEP FOUR** Good Governance Effective Infrastructure • Board Operations	**STEP ONE** Strategic Analysis and Positioning • Mission • Outcomes	
RELATIONSHIPS	**STEP FIVE** Board – Executive Link Board – Director • Structure • Performance Board – Prospective/ New Director • Board Development	**STEP TWO** Direct • Public Regulators • Outcome-driven Relationships Indirect	
RESOURCES	**STEP SIX**	**STEP THREE** Financial Analysis Fund Development • Outcome-driven Resources	
	Board	**SHARED RESPONSIBILITY**	**Management**

STEP SIX
Cost of Good Governance

Resources: Board Level

The board shifts gears to focus on fulfilling its role and how to improve its performance.

The board shifts gears to focus on fulfilling its role and how to improve its performance. What financial resources does it need? This is always a tough question as directors feel guilty taking revenue from operations. However, if there is no discussion and commitment, there is never a change in the way the board functions.

Although directors struggle with defining productive performance, many are hesitant to devote time and money for formal education; so on-the-job training replaces quality instruction. Unfortunately, the chance of a good "learning by doing" experience is rare because there are so many misconceptions about what constitutes governance. Despite the fact that intentions are sincere, this circumstance perpetuates the inevitable. Predictably, it is assumed that past board service guarantees a seasoned, knowledgeable director for the next board commitment. And the cycle continues . . .

Because director education is often overlooked, **BoardSteps** stresses that funding for it must be included in the annual budget. The dollars for training sessions, planning retreats and related activities may come from general funds, from an outside funder, or—most commonly in small organizations—from the directors themselves. Alternatively, some of the funds may be raised in-kind: a leadership consultant or financial professional may donate services; or a technology firm may provide conference-call facilities so all board members may learn about an emergent issue facing the nonprofit.

Some boards insist that they get by with no budget at all since they are "cost neutral." It is probably more accurate to say that organizational resources—staff hours and materials—are used but not measured. In reality, it costs money to nurture, staff and support the board. **BoardSteps** is not about just getting by. It is about succeeding with a common understanding among directors about what constitutes good governance.

In this step, a cost of good governance standard is drafted to reinforce what every director (and funder) knows to be true. If the board wants to do its job better, it must insist that revenue be directed to its education and training. This represents a wise investment that will provide a return to the nonprofit with the increased effectiveness of the board.

Finally, **BoardSteps** encourages a thoughtful appraisal about what specific education, training and support will enhance board performance; then the board identifies resource needs based on results and relationships.

> In this step, a cost of good governance standard is drafted to reinforce the reality.

Cost of Good Governance Standard Example

The board must be a contributor to the mission rather than just a consumer of precious resources. It is imperative that board members have the skills to effectively participate at the governance level and each director must have the opportunity to learn about activities and dynamics that are encompassed in accountability. The board recognizes the costs associated with the necessary education and training to enhance individual involvement in decision making and administrative support to ensure board performance.

Tools to Define Board Resources

Cost of Good Governance Standard ◆ Worksheet 6A

Using Worksheet 6A, directors recognize the need for a standard regarding the cost of good governance.

Resources: Board Level ◆ Worksheet 6B

With 6B, the board looks for the areas where funding is needed, an amount, and a possible funding source.

◆ IN REVIEW...

Step Six will help your board:

◆ Draft a cost of good governance standard, (Worksheet 6A)

◆ Identify areas where financial resources are needed to support good governance (Worksheet 6B),

◆ Establish the cost, and

◆ Determine source of funding.

Every board can benefit from education and training. Recognize that fact and seek the resources to help you improve performance.

The Management Level

BOARDSTEPS			
RESULTS	**STEP FOUR** Good Governance Effective Infrastructure • Board Operations	**STEP ONE** Strategic Analysis and Positioning • Mission • Outcomes	Outstanding Operational Performance
RELATIONSHIPS	**STEP FIVE** Board – Executive Link Board – Director • Structure • Performance Board – Prospective/ New Director • Board Development	**STEP TWO** Direct • Public Regulators • Outcome-driven Relationships Indirect	Executive – Staff Staff – Staff
RESOURCES	**STEP SIX** Cost of Good Governance	**STEP THREE** Financial Analysis Fund Development • Outcome-driven Resources	Financial Management Systems
	Board	**SHARED RESPONSIBILITY**	**Management**

BoardSteps maintains emphasis on the board and its work and does not address the staff side of the governance-management equation. Each nonprofit is unique and the executive is the best designer of systems to maximize available human resources. Ideally, as the board has just done, management will undertake a similar assessment to build and maintain its own infrastructure.

The executive is accountable to the board for all facets of the management area and the staff configuration to accomplish work toward the prioritized organizational outcomes. Management's focus and activities are monitored employing the standards determined in the organizational level: Shared Responsibility steps. These blend with the board's good governance practices to position the nonprofit for success.

There are many available sources regarding management operations and some are noted in Section 3: References.

THE BIG PICTURE

BOARDSTEPS			
RESULTS	**STEP FOUR** **Good Governance** **Effective Infrastructure** • Board Operations	**STEP ONE** **Strategic Analysis** **and Positioning** • Mission • Outcomes	**Outstanding** **Operational** **Performance**
RELATIONSHIPS	**STEP FIVE** **Board – Executive Link** **Board – Director** • Structure • Performance **Board – Prospective/** **New Director** • Board Development	**STEP TWO** Direct • Public Regulators • Outcome-driven Relationships Indirect	**Executive – Staff** **Staff – Staff**
RESOURCES	**STEP SIX** **Cost of Good** **Governance**	**STEP THREE** **Financial Analysis** **Fund Development** • Outcome-driven Resources	**Financial** **Management** **Systems**
	Board	**SHARED** **RESPONSIBILITY**	**Management**
	Board Monitoring		**Management** **Monitoring**
	Board Accountability		

The comprehensive framework above ties both the external and internal steps together. There is a natural sequence that begins with the organization's leadership articulating why the nonprofit exists and what value it adds to the world. It then proceeds to bring more definition to its mission and outcomes by identifying relationships and addressing resources. Finally, the board determines how it will do business to underpin all nonprofit efforts.

1 Results: Organizational Level

◆ Establish the mission (Worksheet 1A),
◆ Assess internal and external opportunities and challenges (Worksheets 1B, 1C),
◆ List desired outcomes (Worksheet 1D), and
◆ Prioritize those outcomes (Worksheet 1E).

The work here creates the foundation upon which all future steps are built.

2 Relationships: Organizational Level

◆ Identify public regulators for your organization (Worksheet 2A),
◆ Develop a legal compliance checklist and schedule (Worksheet 2B), and
◆ Identify relationships based on each prioritized outcome (Worksheet 2C).

The checklist is monitored on the board's regular agenda and the official minutes document compliance. Linking prioritized outcomes and relationships allows the board-executive team to define what interaction is needed, why, and when it should happen.

3 Resources: Organizational Level

◆ Establish the financial management and reporting systems it will use for monitoring (Worksheet 3A), and
◆ Identify potential funders for each prioritized outcome (Worksheet 3B).

Agreement has been reached on the financial management system that provides the board with data it needs to exercise governance oversight. Outcomes are matched with prospects for funding.

4 Results: Board Level

◆ Establish a <u>Statement of Commitment</u> to Good Governance and an Effective Infrastructure (Worksheet 4A),
◆ Assess its internal and external opportunities and challenges (Worksheet 4B, 4C),
◆ Identify the Board Operations Standards Inventory (Worksheet 4D).

The board concentrates on organizing to become an effective part of the board-management equation. In its collective voice it commits to the creation of an infrastructure that underpins its practice of good governance. The organization's Standards Inventory begins to be developed.

5 Relationships: Board Level

◆ Identify its internal relationships,
◆ Establish the broad categories of standards, and
◆ Develop Board-Executive Link, Board Structure, Performance, and Development Standards Inventories **(Worksheets 5A, 5B, 5C)**.

Board relationships—board-executive, board-director, board-prospective/new director—set the stage for the work of the governing body.

6 Resources: Board Level

◆ Draft a cost of good governance standard **(Worksheet 6A)**,
◆ Identify areas where financial resources are needed to support good governance **(Worksheet 6B)**,
◆ Establish the cost, and
◆ Determine the source of funding.

Every board can benefit from education and training. Recognize that fact and seek the resources to help you improve performance.

When a board moves through these six steps, the efforts of the organization become focused and more constructive. Directors are clear on the role they should play and how they relate to the executive and management. A strategic direction is set and progress can be monitored.

Further, the board will be confident that it is a positive contributor to the organization and to the community, and accountable to the public.

Standards, Worksheets, and References

Writing Standards

Speaking in its *collective voice,* the board expresses the standards it will use to govern both organizational and board level activities. To reiterate, a standard is the board's final word about what it expects to happen over a certain period of time. It measures individual and organizational behavior according to clear, familiar concepts: quantity, quality and degree. Standards are the rules by which the organization, board and staff conduct business.

As the board walks through the **BoardSteps** steps, I recommend that it appoint a board recorder to capture its conversation and document where it wants standards to guide decisions. By waiting until the completion of all worksheets, the board will have a better understanding of how to use standards and its monitoring schedule.

An ad hoc workgroup is charged with drafting standards that will be presented to the board for its consideration and adoption. The record of the board's discussion forms the substance of the writing process.

Organizing Standards

A nonprofit's governing documents are arranged in a logical order beginning with the articles of incorporation, then bylaws and organizational standards. The board methodically moves through the six steps of the framework to organize its standards inventory. Beginning with Results: Shared Responsibility suggested standards might read like the following ones.

The board of (nonprofit name) will:

◆ Use **BoardSteps** to establish a system of good governance to guide organizational decisions and demonstrate accountability to the public.

◆ Govern by first focusing on the Shared Responsibility area where it collaborates with management to determine strategic direction.

Speaking in its collective voice, the board expresses the standards it will use to govern both organizational and board level activities.

◆ Engage in strategic analysis and positioning to clarify what the organization will achieve, in what context, and for what reasons.

Next, the board documents the standards of mission and outcomes. Though these broad statements may seem insufficient for monitoring, keep in mind that they represent the beginning of the standards-writing process. For each outcome, the board continues to write more detail until it is comfortable that the statement is measurable and it can gauge progress.

Directors must maintain an awareness of the different levels of standards in an organization. The board concerns itself with organizational standards, while the executive writes operational standards. It is the board's prerogative to decide when it has given adequate direction for management's decisions. The hand-off point will differ from nonprofit to nonprofit, board to board but it will eventually be reached. At this junction, the board has outlined what it will use to measure organizational performance. The executive then develops operational standards that influence day-to-day staff activities.

Monitoring Standards

When the Standards Inventory is complete, it is monitored on a regular basis. Every standard is scheduled for monitoring at least once a year on the board's annual calendar. The most efficient way to accomplish this is by linking meeting business with the relevant standards. For example:

◆ Financial analysis standards are monitored when financials are presented.

◆ Board Resources standards are reviewed before budget development to determine board revenue requirements.

◆ Board and director performances are evaluated using the board level relationship standards before each yearly planning retreat.

Executive performance is directly tied to organizational performance and is measured by the standards set by the board. Shared Responsibility standards are monitored to determine progress toward pre-determined organizational outcomes within the established legal, ethical and financial boundaries. Board-Executive Link standards are reviewed to make sure the executive is meeting board expectations. These are the board's tools to evaluate performance.

The incident of noncompliance or violation of any standard must be documented in the meeting minutes along with the board's plan for future monitoring to ensure compliance. In this way, the board demonstrates that it is aware of what is happening and has set a course of action without micromanaging.

By working through each step of the **BoardSteps** framework and developing applicable standards, the board has a greater appreciation of its job and how to proactively govern the organization. Directors experience great satisfaction in working together to keep the nonprofit focused on its outcomes, sound in its finances, ethical and efficient in its operations, and vibrant in its capacity to address change and growth. Now, the board adds value to its organization and to its community.

Developing the Standards Inventory

Each board will create its inventory taking into consideration its specific circumstances. A sample Standards Inventory is presented on the following pages. Some of the suggested groupings will be expanded or eliminated and others will be added to the list as the board reaches consensus about what it has to say.

When the board is satisfied that it has created the appropriate checks and balances system, it governs the organization with confidence.

Sample STANDARDS INVENTORY

1. Results: Organizational Level
  A. Implementation of **BoardSteps**
  B. Recognition of Shared Responsibility Area
  C. Strategic Analysis and Positioning
  D. Mission
  E. Prioritized Outcomes

2. Relationships: Organizational Level
  A. Direct Relationships
    1. Public Regulators
      • Identification
      • Legal Compliance Checklist and Schedule
    <u>Outcome-driven Relationships</u>
    2. Funders
      • Identification of Outcome-driven Funding Need
    3. Clients
      • Definition of Client
      • Service Delivery
      • Risk Management
    4. Volunteers
      • Definition of Volunteer
      • Volunteer Management
    5. Members
      • Definition of Member
      • Parent-Member Relationship
      • Authority and Accountability
    6. Collaborators
      • Purpose of Collaboration
      • Participation Criteria
      • Roles of Participants
    7. Third-party Professionals
      • Selection
      • Reporting
    8. News Media
      • Interaction Process
  B. Indirect Relationships
      • Identification
      • Communication

3. Resources: Organizational Level
  A. Financial Analysis
      • Financial Management Systems
      • Financial Planning
      • Financial Conditions
      • Financial Reporting
      • Asset Protection
      • Investments
  B. Fund Development
    <u>Outcome-driven Resources</u>
      • Identification of Potential Funder
      • Maintenance of Funder Relationship
      • Reporting and Compliance

Sample STANDARDS INVENTORY

4. Results: Board Level
A. Good Governance
B. Effective Infrastructure
  1. Board Operations
     - Annual Board Calendar
     - Board Meetings
     - Agendas
     - Legal Records (minutes, audits, etc.)
     - Planning Retreats
     - Executive Sessions
     - Issues Education
     - Standards Inventory
     - Monitoring Mechanism and Schedule
     - Liability: D & O Insurance
     - Use of Third-party Professionals

5. Relationships: Board Level
A. Board-Executive Link
   - Search and Selection
   - Compensation and Benefits
   - Delegation
   - Support for Executive
   - Performance Evaluation
   - Dismissal
   - Interim Executive Plan
   - Communication with the Executive
   - Board Relationship with Staff
   - Directors Relationship with Staff
   - Directors as Management Volunteers

B. Executive-Board Link
   - Reporting to Board
   - Communication with the Board
   - Crisis Management Plan
   - Relationship with Individual Directors
   - Support to the Board and Individual Directors

C. Board-Director
   1. Board Structure
      - Chair
      - Workgroups
      - Officers and Officers Authority
   2. Board Performance
      - Statement of Commitment
      - Collective Voice Philosophy
      - Conflict of Interest
      - Performance Assessment
   3. Individual Director Performance
      - Standards of Conduct
      - Performance Assessment
D. Director-Prospective/New Director
   1. Board Development
      - Board Development Plan
      - Recruitment
      - Nomination, Election
      - Orientation
      - Mentoring
      - Education and Training
      - Leadership Development

6. Resources: Board Level
A. Cost of Good Governance
B. Identification of Needed Resources
   - Board Operations
   - Board Structure
   - Director Performance
   - Board Development

Worksheets
The following worksheets support the board's work utilizing BoardSteps.

Mission of the Organization

A mission statement drives all decision making for the nonprofit.
It expresses why the organization exists.
It states the organization's primary purpose or reason for being.

Our mission statement articulates *WHY we do WHAT we do.*

The mission statement should answer the following questions:

Why does our organization exist?

What is the difference we are trying to make?

For whom?

If your organization already has a mission statement, is it:

☐ *Realistic?* ☐ *Clear?* ☐ *Concise?* ☐ *Persuasive?*

The answer to these should be a resounding "yes" before proceeding.

External Scan: The Wider World

What is happening outside our organization
that could affect our ability to achieve our mission?

External Trend	Potential Impact		Additional Information What more do we need to know?
	Is it a PLUS? Opportunity	Is it a MINUS? Challenge	

Internal Scan: A Look Inside Our Organization

What is happening inside our organization
that could affect our ability to achieve our mission?

Internal Trend	Potential Impact		Additional Information What more do we need to know?
	Is it a PLUS? Opportunity	**Is it a MINUS?** Challenge	

Organizational Outcomes

What outcomes will support our mission?

STEP ONE: RESULTS	ORGANIZATIONAL LEVEL	WORKSHEET 1E

Prioritization of Organizational Outcomes

Where do we want to focus our organizational energy?
Prioritize the Organizational Outcomes from Worksheet 1D, beginning with the most important.

Organizational Outcome
(1)
(2)
(3)
(4)
(5)
(6)

Organizational Relationships: Public Regulators

To which public and semi-public regulators must the organization relate?

Government:

    (1) Federal

    (2) State

    (3) Municipal

    (4) Other

Accreditors:

    (1) Government-affiliated

    (2) Private (professional or industry associations)

    (3) Voluntary/optional (i.e. "watchdog" groups)

    (4) Other

    (5) Other

Legal Compliance Checklist and Schedule
To be completed with the assistance of a third-party professional

What compliance measures must the organization take?
Who will be responsible for each compliance task?

Public Regulator	Legal Requirement	Documentation Who? By When?	Compliance Who? By When?	Reporting Action/Schedule Who? By When?
Secretary of State				
Federal (IRS)				
Federal				
State				
Municipal				

Outcome-driven
Organizational Relationships

What relationships are necessary to achieve the desired outcome?

Organizational outcome: _____

From Worksheet 1E — *Copy this worksheet for each outcome.*

Relationship (Client, funder, collaborator, etc.)	Is this a director/ board interaction?		Is this a management interaction?	What is the shared responsibility?	Purpose of Action	Action will take place by...
	Director Who?	Board	Who?			
				Director/Board		
				Staff		
				Director/Board		
				Staff		
				Director/Board		
				Staff		
				Director/Board		
				Staff		
Coordinated by	**Board Chair**		**Executive**			

Financial Analysis
Board Discussion Notes

Each board will approach financial analysis from its own unique position. A facilitated discussion is necessary to focus the board and executive on what is needed for responsible oversight. A board workgroup may be charged with this work and it begins with this worksheet.

BOARD MEMBERS:	Yes	No
Understand all financial statements.		
Believe that current financials provide accurate and timely information for responsible oversight.		
Believe systems need to be redesigned.		
Wish to engage an outside professional.		
Would benefit from financial training.		

Identification of Categories of Financial Analysis Standards

In its collective voice, the board identifies the categories of standards it wants developed and documents *any* specific concerns regarding financial oversight. Using this information, a board workgroup can draft standards for the board's consideration.

Some category suggestions include:
Financial Planning
Financial Conditions
Asset Protection
Budgeting
Investments
Other
Specific concerns

Outcome-driven Funder Identification

Who Will Support the Work Necessary to Achieve This Organizational Outcome?

Organizational outcome: _____

Building on Worksheets 1E and 2C — *Copy this worksheet for each outcome.*

Potential Funder	Is this a director/ board interaction?		Is this a staff interaction?	What is the shared responsibility?	To what end? Anticipated result of action	Action will take place by...
	Director Who?	Board	Who?			
Government				Director/Board		
				Staff		
Foundation				Director/Board		
				Staff		
Corporation				Director/Board		
				Staff		
Individuals				Director/Board		
				Staff		
Other				Director/Board		
				Staff		
Coordinated by	**Board Chair**		**Executive**			

GOOD GOVERNANCE is the *primary result* the board seeks.
The *second result* is the development of an effective
infrastructure to support the board's work.

Statement of Commitment to Good Governance

External Scan: Outside the Boardroom

What is happening *outside* the boardroom that could
affect the board's ability to practice good government?

External Trend	Potential Impact		Additional Information What more do we need to know?
	Is it a PLUS? Opportunity	**Is it a MINUS?** Challenge	

Internal Scan: A Look At The Board

What is happening *within* the board that could
affect its ability to practice good governance?

Internal Trend	Potential Impact		Additional Information What more do we need to know?
	Is it a PLUS? Opportunity	Is it a MINUS? Challenge	

Board Operations Standards

In its collective voice, the board says how it will conduct its business
and develop an inventory of Board Operations Standards.

Standards Inventory	Specific Comments
Board Operations	
Annual Board Calendar	
Board Meetings	
Agendas	
Legal Records (Minutes, Audits)	
Planning Retreats	
Executive Sessions	
Issues Education	
Standards Inventory	
Monitoring Mechanism	
Monitoring Schedule	
Liability	
• Directors and Officers Liability Insurance	
• Indemnification	
Use of Third Party Professionals	
•	

Relationships: Board – Executive

Under each category, board-executive and executive-board, an inventory of standards is developed to bring more definition to the relationship and allow for monitoring.

Standards Inventory	Specific Comments
Board – Executive Link	
Search and Selection	
Compensation & Benefits	
Delegation	
Support for Executive	
Performance Evaluation	
Dismissal	
Interim Executive Plan	
Communication with the Executive	
Board Relationship with Staff	
Directors Relationship with Staff	
Directors as Management Volunteers	
•	
•	
•	
Executive – Board Link	
Reporting to Board	
Communication with the Board	
Crisis Management Plan	
Relationship with Individual Directors	
Support to Board	
Support to Individual Director	
•	
•	

Relationships: Board - Director

Board Structure, Board and Individual Director Performance Categories
are expanded with the development of an inventory.

Standards Inventory	Specific Comments

Board Structure
Chair
Workgroups
• Executive Committee
• Standing Committees
• Ad hocs
Officers
Officers' Authority
•
 	
Board Performance
Statement of Commitment
Collective Voice Philosophy
Conflict of Interest
Fund Development Performance
Collective Performance Assessment
•
 	
Individual Director Performance
Standards of Conduct
Individual Performance Assessment
• Attendance
• Fund Development
  • Participation
  • Financial Contribution
  • Event Presence
•	

Relationships:
Director – Prospective/New Director

The board determines how it will perpetuate itself and continually provide education at the board table and training for new directors.

Standards Inventory	Specific Comments
Board Development	
Board Development Plan	
• Skills Assessment	
• Skills Identification	
•	
•	
•	
Recruitment	
Nomination	
Election	
Orientation	
Mentoring	
Education and Training	
Leadership Development	
•	
•	

Resources: Board Level

The board has made a commitment to practice good governance in Step Four.
It must fulfill that promise to the organization and the public. It recognized that
commitment through a standard regarding the cost of good governance.

Cost of Good Governance Standard

Resources: Board Level

What revenue does the board need to do its job
and improve its performance around the board table?

Results	Budget Amount	Source of Funding
Board Operations		
Board Meetings		
• Administrative Support		
• Issues Education		
Planning Retreats		
• Administrative Support		
• Research Needs		
Directors and Officers Liability Insurance		
Third Party Professional Fees		
Relationships		
Board Structure		
Administrative Support for:		
• Chair		
• Board Workgroups		
• Officers		
•		
Director Performance		
Fund Development Support		
•		
Board Development		
Recruitment		
Orientation		
Governance Training		
Speaker's Fund		
Meeting Registrations		
Travel Expenses		

References

The following books and publications provide valuable insights and information about nonprofit governance and management. As your organization works through the **BoardSteps** framework, you may find it useful to consult them.

Angelica, Marion Peters. *Keeping the Peace, Resolving Conflict in the Boardroom.* St. Paul, Minnesota: Amherst H. Wilder Foundation. 2000.

Annison, Michael. *Managing the Whirlwind.* Englewood, CO: Medical Group Management Association Publishers. 1993.

Annison, Michael, and Dan S. Wilford. *Trust Matters, New Directions in Health Care Leadership.* San Francisco: Jossey-Bass Publishers. 1998.

BoardSource. *The Nonprofit Governance Index.* Washington, DC: BoardSource (formerly the National Center for Nonprofit Boards). 2002.

Board Member. "The Periodical for Members of BoardSource." Washington, DC: BoardSource. *Board Member* is published eight times a year.

Bowen, William G. *Inside the Boardroom, Governance by Directors and Trustees.* New York: John Wiley & Sons, Inc. 1994.

Burstein, Joann Morgan. *Not-for-profit Board of Directors Manual.* Metro Volunteers! Denver. 2000.

Carver, John. *Boards That Make a Difference: A New Design for Leadership in Nonprofit and Public Organizations.* San Francisco: Jossey-Bass Publishers, 1990.

Carver, John, and Miriam Mayhew Carver. *Reinventing Your Board.* San Francisco: Jossey-Bass Publishers. 1997.

Drucker, Peter F. *The Drucker Foundation Self-Assessment Tool.* New York: Jossey-Bass Publishers. 1999.

Fram, Eugene H., and Vicki Brown. *Policy vs. Paper Clips: Selling the Corporate Model to Your Nonprofit Board.* Second Ed. Milwaukee: Families International, Inc. 1995.

Hall, Peter D. *Inventing the NonProfit Sector and Other Essays on Philanthropy, Voluntarism, and NonProfit Organizations.* Baltimore: Johns Hopkins University Press. 1992.

Hesselbein, Frances, Marshall Goldsmith and Richard Beckhard. *The Leader of the Future.* San Franciso: Jossey-Bass Publishers. 1996.

Oliver, Caroline, General Ed., with Mike Conduff, et al. *The Policy Governance Field Book.* San Francisco: Jossey-Bass Publishers. 1999.

Overton, George W., Ed. *Guidebook for Directors of Nonprofit Organizations. Section of Business Law, American Bar Association.* Chicago: American Bar Association. 1993.

Zall, Ronald I., Esquire. *The Director's Handbook: A Guide for Directors of Privately Held Corporations.* Washington, DC: National Association of Corporate Directors. 1996.

There are many websites regarding the work of the nonprofit sector. To name a few:

boardsource.org

mapnp.org

independentsector.org

irs.ustreas.gov

compasspoint.org

arnova.org

carvergovernance.com

BoardSteps
Board Job Description

A. Position Title: Director

Length of Term:
Responsible to: Entire board
Time Commitment:
Purpose: As a collective body, the board governs the nonprofit, ensures adherence to all laws, and is accountable to the public for all organizational actions.

B. Governance Duties

Results

The board determines the strategic direction, defines the mission, and prioritizes the organizational outcomes of the nonprofit.

Relationships

The board preserves and nurtures a number of external and internal relationships to ensure the accomplishment of mission and outcomes.

Resources

The board secures the financial resources to sustain the organization and oversees their proper management.

Monitoring

The board demonstrates accountability by establishing standards to measure both organizational and board performance. It monitors its standards inventory on a regular schedule to ensure compliance.

C. Individual Director Expectations

Time
- ◆ Attend all board and work group meetings
- ◆ Be willing to assume leadership positions
- ◆ Prepare adequately for meetings in order to make informed decisions

Fund Development
- ◆ Fulfill fund development role
- ◆ Make an annual gift

Board Continuity
- ◆ Support the board development function
- ◆ Champion ongoing board training and education

Acknowledgments

Since the beginning of this project I have benefited from the wise counsel of Janet Unger, President of Unger Consulting Services. Janet and I are both graduates of The Carver Policy Governance® Academy, and that experience brought us together as colleagues and as friends. Our shared knowledge of "Carver" provided a springboard for many of our discussions. Over the past two years, Janet has endured endless drafts of this work with patience and grace. I sincerely appreciate her excellent advice and continuing support as I have defined the fundamentals of the **BoardSteps** framework.

For almost three decades, the dissemination of John Carver's work has generated tremendous discussion about nonprofit governance. John and his wife, Miriam, deserve the thanks of the sector for bringing this topic to the forefront. They rarely get the praise they should for their efforts. Their lifelong dedication to improving the quality of board service must be applauded.

Sometimes the act of capturing thoughts on paper can be both time-consuming and downright frustrating. To Fran McElhill, Boyd Morgan, Matt Rubin, Michael Annison, Mary Helms, Anne Greene, Tyleta Morgan and Lynne Moore Siegel—thank you for your editing suggestions that smoothed the way.

Chris Speranza worked diligently to help get this book into a final form. I fondly refer to her as the grammar police because her command of grammar and language has always astounded me. She was always willing to spend entire days by my side weighing the intent of every word. Praise, cheers and standing ovations are well deserved.

Finally, I'm very grateful to Phil, John and Alli for encouraging me to write this book and reading it multiple times. Thank you for your love and support, and for being the best family ever!

About the Author

Joann Morgan Burstein, President of Nonprofit Board Advisors, specializes in board governance. With fifteen years of consulting and twenty-five years of board experience, she serves a diverse portfolio of clients from struggling grassroots nonprofits to established multimillion-dollar organizations. She bases her practice on the principle that good governance strengthens organizational performance.

Ms. Burstein divides her time between Denver and Philadelphia. Her leadership commitments over the years include service on the boards of an international women's association, independent school, women's foundation, AIDS project, city-wide corporate giving program, maternal substance abuse pilot, mayor's welfare reform initiative, and most recently, a maternal care coalition. As president of the boards of the Mile High Transplant Bank, Junior League of Denver, Metro Volunteers, and JLD Foundation, she led each organization with clarity of purpose and focus on the governing role.

Her career path encompasses work as a staffer for an inner city drug treatment program, a full-time mother, community volunteer, travel planner, fundraiser and consultant. She was employed as a hospital pharmacist at the Medical College of Virginia, staff facilitator and training coordinator at the Denver Museum of Natural History, and consulting associate for LaSalle University's Nonprofit Center in Philadelphia.

Ms. Burstein participates in national meetings and training courses, including BoardSource, The Carver Policy Governance® Academy, and LaSalle's Nonprofit Center. For the past three years, she has devoted her time to the writing of *BoardSteps* — the culmination of her resolve to design an easily understood governance system for nonprofit boards.

Nonprofit Board Advisors, LLC
1820 Rittenhouse Square, Suite 1102 • *Philadelphia, PA 19103*
215-893-7887

www.boardsteps.com